TALES OF LIECHTENSTEIN

THEN AND NOW

by

JAMES FOSTER ROBINSON

Dedicated to the Prince and Princess and the people of

Liechtenstein

CONTENTS

INTRODUCTION

Those who have heard of the Principality of Liechtenstein think of it as a fairy tale kingdom. But the little country is real! Only about eleven miles long and six miles wide, it sits on the east bank of the Upper Rhine River across from Switzerland. Its eastern border is the mountain range that separates it from Austria.

Its people have big hearts and their history is long and adventurous. This small alpine nation sits on the Upper Rhine at the crossroads of History. Romans, Celts, Franks, Huns, Arabs, Germans, Swiss, Swedes are just a few of the many people who have passed through and fought, lived and died in this amazing little land. Its people have survived wars, invasions, floods, plague, avalanches, starvation, despotic and indifferent rulers and have even flourished. Today they have one of the highest incomes per capita in the world.

I have never been to Liechtenstein but I have met a family of four from there when they were visiting Vancouver, BC, in the summer of 2000. I dream of visiting it some day. So far, fate and misfortune have never allowed me to accomplish my dream. Perhaps next year in Liechtenstein!

Liechtenstein and the surrounding countries have many tales to tell. I have researched the country's history, tales and legends. This is a collection of some of those legends, tall tales and true stories. I have gathered some them from various sources and have written one of my own. The material in this book has been published previously by myself on Suite101.com or is from my unpublished manuscript "A History of Liechtenstein". There are many, many more stories that could be told about this amazing Principality. In my own humble words, I now present some tales of Liechtenstein, then and now. I hope you enjoy them!

James Foster Robinson
May/June 2014

West Virginia, USA

THEN

THE DEVIL IN LIECHTENSTEIN

Image in public domain as per http://aboutfacts.net/Mysterious85.html

THE DEVIL YOKE (DAS TEUFELSJOCH)

In an area in Switzerland near Sax and Gams, there is a cliff on a mountain on the left bank of the Rhine opposite Feldkirch that can be seen from the north end of Liechtenstein particularly at the Parish of Bendern. There is a hole in the center of that cliff that when the sun is in the right position and shines through that hole, it appears to be like a golden sheaf or eye. This phenomenoin is called the Devil's Yoke.

THE DEVIL'S HOLE

A farmer living in Liechtenstein thought he could not get his crops in in time so he made a deal with the devil. He would sell his soul to the devil if the devil could get all his crops in before the evening ringing of the bell at the local church. The devil agreed and set to work. He was almost done and had only one more sheaf to tie up when, to his chagrin, the bell in the local church rang out. The devil was so irate that he had lost a soul that he picked up a pointed tree and flung it with such violence that it flew across the Rhine and drove into the side of a mountain causing a big hole. That hole is still called the devil's hole.

THE DEVIL WEARING BELLS (DER GLOCKENTRAGENDE TEUFEL)

In a chapel in the small community of Masescha at Triesnerberg, there is a scene or statues on the left hand of the alter. One shows a young blonde and beardless bishop. Next to him is the devil with the right foot ending in a grasping claw , the left foot in a cloven hoof and around its neck is a bell. How did the devil come to be wearing a bell?

St. Theodule or Theodore, as some others call him, was Bishop of Sion in Valais in the 6th Century. Today he is the patron saint of that community. They celebrate his memory on August 16 every year.

Back then, the pope gave Saint Theodule a big bell as a gift. Saint Theodule had recently expelled the devil from a possessed man and when he saw him again, he forced the devil to wear that big bell over the alps all the way to

Masescha.

THE DEVIL'S STONE

The Devil's Stone above the village of Triesen in Liechtenstein gets it name from what was said to have occurred there during the Middle Ages. The infamous witch-hunt, where over 300 citizens of Liechtenstein were accused witchcraft and burnt at the stake, was centered on this village. Old Roman sulfur baths used to exist in the mountains above the village and were said to be the scene of wild orgies by Satan's followers. The well and the buildings have long disappeared but a big stone remains. The stone bears marks like the imprint of a goat's hoof. Thus it has become known as "Devil's Stone".

THE WHITE HORSE OF LOCHGASS

Once there was a greedy farmer who lived on the Lochgass Road in Vaduz. He was well known for his stealing of anything that he could get his hands on, especially horses. One Christmas Eve, he was roaming about looking for something to borrow permanently when he spied a white saddled horse tied up outside a church across the Rhine in Switzerland. Immediately he mount the horse and lit out for Vaduz. That horse started to race so fast that the thief could hardly hold on. When the horse reached the Lochgass, it stopped suddenly, throwing the man to the ground and breaking his neck. As the thief lay there dying, he saw to his sorrow the white horse turn into the devil. Hence forth, the thief was condemned to ride up and down the Lochgass Road as a white horse. Luckily for him, he was released from his nightmare when the good citizens of the area erected a cross on the road. The old Lochgass Road is now known as The "Schimmelgasse" ("White Horse Road").

THE GUSCHG HERDSMEN' DOLL

There is an alpine meadow up in the Guschg region of the Valorschtal Valley near Schaan. There a small group of shepherds and herdsmen who stayed in in a lonely cabin. They got bored and one day made a life-sized female doll and treated it as if it was human. They spoke to it, eat with it among other things and even beat it when they were in a foul mood.

Then, in the autumn, it was time to move the sheep and cattle to winter pastures below. Amazingly, that rag doll sat up and began to talk to the men. They were of course very frightened. Wouldn't you be if a doll that you made began to talk? It told them that all of of them but one could leave with the animals. That one had to stay with her. Then she pointed to one of the men. The rest of them quickly gathered their stuff and took the herds down the mountain. A little ways down, they turned and looked back at the cabin. There on the roof was the doll laughing and sitting beside the skin of the chosen herdsman stretched across the roof. The other men fled!

WITCHES

Harrison Weir (1824-1906)
This picture is in the public domain as per http://commons.wikimedia.org/wiki/File:
Friendly_Witch_Drawing.jpg

DIE BUNDHAKEN

Once a farmer near Schaan was having trouble with his butter making bucket. No matter how he tried, it just would not make butter. The man was very suspicious and thought he knew what what wrong. He dropped two hot hooks in the bucket and there was plenty of butter all of a sudden. Then his suspicions were confirmed when a neighbor woman came and asked for some cream to put on her hands which appeared to be burnt straight through by hooks. She was, of course, a witch and had cursed his butter bucket.

THE FINGERS BURNED (DEN FINGER VERBRANN)

Some years ago in Balzers, a woman tried to open her butter tubs but they would not open. Her husband sitting a table picked up a straw and stuck in the flame of a candle. The tube immediately came loose. The next day a neighbor's daughter came and asked for some butter for her mother who had mysteriously burnt her fingers. Many believed that the woman with the burnt fingers was a witch who had put a spell on the butter tubs.

THE JOURNAL ILGEN (DAS ILGENBLATT)

They tell the story in Balzars, Liechtenstein, of a poor man who had a rich brother who was stingy with his wealth. The rich brother refused to share with the poor brother who was reduced to begging. This poor brother was living in a miserable cabin in the mountains when a huge flock of magpies flew into the hut. Now these magpies or Agersten were actually witches. Ignoring the poor man, they started chatting about all sorts of things. One magpie told about a king's daughter who was very sick and no doctor could cure her. One of the witches - sorry magpies - remarked that she could be cured by placing a certain type of leaf on her temple. Well that poor man heard that and knew where to find such a leaf. He quickly procured it and grabbing the ear of one of the birds was transported to the king's palace. There he presented himself as a doctor and promised to cure the princess. He placed the leaf on the girl's temple, and like the magpie said, she was cured. The poor man, now richly rewarded, traveled on. The other brother, hearing his poor brother's story but apparently not listening to the whole thing, decided to travel to court and become a doctor there. Can you guess what happened? That is right! The rich brother was turned down and sent away in shame.

THE WITCH HUNTS

Public domain image as per http://www.examiner.com/article/harry-potter-and-the-search-for-superstition-witch-hunting-africa

In the 1660's, after plague had scoured the valley, witch hunting added to the horror and misery of the people. Like the rest of Europe, the little county had succumbed to the mass hysteria of suspicion and accusations of witchcraft against neighbors, family and friends. The people, brutalized by hardships, had become use to cruelty and horror. Their minds began to seek dark explanations for the drought, bad harvests, sickness, sudden death or fire. They looked at their neighbors who appeared not to have suffered the same misfortunes and whispered "witchcraft". As always, there were those who were quick to take advantage and soon the whispers became outraged cries.

Under pressure from the local population the judges of the County of Vaduz sought permission to look into the problem. The moment that permission was granted, accusations flooded in. Families were torn apart. Neighbors settled old grudges with cries of witchcraft. The disease spread and few were immune. In the beginning, the judges were lenient but the populace were not satisfied. They hungered for vengeance and threatened rebellion if the judges did not do more in the fight against the evils of witchcraft. The judges, in fear of their own safety, took harsher measures. Torture and execution became common. Swept up in the mania, many confessed rather than face prolonged torture. The flames grew higher.

A flat grassy meadow between Steg and the Samina valley called the Hahnenspiel was where witches were said to gather after midnight to dance and generally carry on in the way of witches. Other places were also shunned as meeting places of the devil and his followers. Witches also gathered at the high Heuberg above Triesen where they dance with "Fitzli Butzli", the devil dressed in a green coat. In Vaduz itself, there once existed a great lime tree where witches were said to dance with their evil lord.

Whole families were burned or beheaded as it was thought back then that witchcraft was hereditary. In August of 1648, 14 unfortunate souls were executed in the Vaduz. In 1668, the Faehrmann Spiegler, owner of the ferry at Ruggell was accused and executed.

The situation was so bad in Liechtenstein that there was even a group who made it their business to draw up list of people they disliked and accused them of witchcraft. They were called the Brenner, or burners. Based in Triesenberg and Triesen, they spread out across the little land seeking victims. It seems one important requirement to be branded a witch was to have substantial property. Apparently, the property of executed witches was divided up among the accusers. The Brenner grew richer with each burning or beheading.

The priest at Triesen is credited with ending the Brenner's reign of terror. The burners had gotten so bold in their endeavors that they even targeted the priesthood, especially those of the clergy who spoke out against them. One day, they paid a visit to the priest at Triesen. Suspecting that they were up to no good, he invited them in and plied them with wine spiked with a narcotic drug until they all fell fast asleep. Searching them, he found a list of local victims. The pesky priest's name was at the top of the list. This would not do so the priest alerted all the other victims to their pending fate. The victims on the list quickly bound the Brenner and turned then over to the authorities for prosecution and punishment. Many of the families, who were ruined when relatives had been executed, got their property back. The witchcraft horror ended and the people returned to some semblance of sanity.

Local folklore says that God also punished the Brenner for their misdeeds. They were not cast into hell but were banned to a cave now called the Cave of the Tobelhocker in a gorge or Tobel off the road high up the Lawena-Tal or Lawena Alp behind the village of Triesen. In the cave, there are stone tables, at which, local legend says, the souls of the Tobelhocker that have been condemned to sit until judgement day. Because of their stony and merciless hearts when they condemned innocent victims to burning at the stake as witches, they must sit in silence never to speak another lie. Their descendants are cursed to the 9th generation and some Liechtensteiners are reluctant to marry anyone from the Brenner families.

It is hard to comprehend the effect that witchcraft frenzy had on this little country but the following statistics will give you an idea of the extent. Some experts estimate that between the years 1400 and 1700, that at least 110,000 people in Europe were prosecuted for witchcraft and 60,000 executed. Other experts feel that the toll was even higher. In Switzerland, in the 1600's, 8,800 people out of a population on 1,000,000 were put on trial and 4,000 to 5,000 executed. That is about .005 of the population. Austria at the same time executed 1,500 of its population of 2,000,000. That is about .00075. In Liechtenstein, 300 out of 3000 people living there were put to death for witchcraft. This is an astounding .10 or ten percent of the population. It would be like having one out of every 100 people in your community executed.

The horrors of that time, with the plagues, war, famine and misery still linger in the memory of the people of Liechtenstein. Eventually it may fade - maybe!

THE LITTLE PEOPLE

Once upon a time, there lived in the caves near the Alp Sareis above Malbun and Steg in the mountains of Liechtenstein a race of little wild men known as Wildemannli. Shy creatures thickly covered with hair, they loved to help their fellow men. They would come down in the evenings and finish any farm work left by the peasants. In the morning the farmers would find the animals fed and the stables cleaned. They did not come down during bad weather or the Fohn, the hot wind that flowed up from the south at certain times of the year.

The Wildemannli have disappeared and their home is vacant. There is a cave up on the slopes of the Ochsenkopf which looks quite like a church and is still known as the Wildmannakirchli.

A clue to their disappearance may be contained in the next story.

One wild Wildemannli lived on Profatscheng at Schaan where the locals herded cattle. The people seeing him naked especially in the cold winter pitied him and gave him some clothing. The creature told his benefactors "Wild Ma Chleid net lida cha. " I am not sure what that means but the little wild man ran away and never returned. I wonder if the creature was like the house elf in Harry potter books and movies. When given clothing, the house elf were set free. Maybe the wild man was set free by the gift of clothing!

MIRACLES

SANT AMERTA

Back in early Christian times, the village of Triesen was once a beautiful Roman city called Trison. But the people who lived there were mostly wicked. Then one day, God's wrath fell on them. An angel carrying a fiery sword flew over the wicked city calling out ***"Who wants to escape the sinking , flee tions Sant Amerta ! ".***

Alas, only one woman heeded the warning. Leaving her two children at home to play, she went to the church and knelt in prayer. Suddenly a terrible roaring noise startled her. Rushing to the church door, she saw that the whole city was being destroyed by a Rüfi or rock slide. Horrified and not knowing what to do or if her children were safe, she went back into the chapel and prayed again.

When she ventures out again, she found everything was destroyed - except for one building! Her home! It stood untouched! She rushed to it and found her children safe inside sitting by a carving of the Virgin Mary. They say that that house stood there for many years and may still be there.

Today, in memory of this miracle, the chapel of Sant - Amerta stands on a hill above the village.

DIASTERS

"High above the young Rhine lies Liechtenstein"; sing the citizens of Liechtenstein in their "Liechtensteinische Landeshymne" (Liechtenstein National Anthem) to the tune of "God Save The Queen". Throughout their history, the Rhine has been both their friend and enemy. Liechtensteiners used to have a saying that the three greatest headaches for their country were the Rufen (rock slides), the Reblaus(a vine eating insect) and the Rhine. Many people view the Rhine as romantic but along the Liechtenstein border, it is a shallow torrent flowing between high stone banks that prevent flooding in the spring.

The Rhine is born high up in the Alps in the Rheinwaldhorn Glacier of Switzerland flowing northwards 1,320 km (820 miles) to the North Sea. The name Rhine comes from the Celtic word "renos" that translates as "raging flow". The western third of Liechtenstein lies along the flood plain of Rhine that forms the border with Switzerland for 27 kilometres from Balzers in the south to Ruggell in the north. To the east lies the Rhatikonassif, a part of the central Alps, rising more than 2,438 meters (8,000 feet) above sea level.

The castle of Gutenberg is perched on a big rock at Balzars. Years ago, the Rhine used to come right up to its base on the west and north side while a marshy lake lay on its east and south side. This natural fortress protected the road from Italy to Germany by the Luzienass and the Upper Rhine valley.

In the Schaan area of the Rhine, the land used to be swampy and often flooded by the Rhine. Much of the land was reclaimed when a canal was built. For centuries, much of the low-lying Rhine valley was useless swamp. Eventually over 2,500 acres were drained and used for farming by the construction of dikes and skillful irrigation.

Near the villages of Schaan and Eschen, the Escheuns river flows through marshy meadows where a lake once existed.

Ruggell, the most low-lying commune in Liechtenstein (430 m above sea level) lies on the edge of the Eschnerberg in the flat Rhine valley plain. Until the 19th century, the village was subject to the wild whims of the Rhine and devastated by its frequent floods. Except for the high ground of the Eschnerberg, the whole area was swamp. When Swiss farmers across the river in St. Gallen built dikes, the floods became worse.

For thousands of years, the peasants of Liechtenstein suffered repeatedly from the Rhine's flooding. Since the Liechtenstein family purchased the two counties in the early 1700's, which became the present day Principality, disastrous floods occurred in 1739, 1762, 1775, 1785, 1789, 1816, 1817, 1821, 1839, 1846 and 1855.

In 1846, the Rhine River flooded the Liechtenstein valley for six weeks. Two hundred and fifty people fled the ensuing famine for a better life in America. Those who remained suffered much hardship. Prince Alois, visiting his Principality for the second time, was appalled at the devastation and gave orders to his officials to try and prevent further flooding. The local administrators had the riverbank fortified, dams built and swamps drained. As a result, many acres of good land in the Lowlands were reclaimed for farming.

Previously, ferryboats were the only means to cross the river. Wooden bridges were built at Balzers, Vaduz, Schaan and Bendern between 1865 and 1870. By 1970, the wooden bridges at Schaan on the Zurich-Vienna road, and at Balzers and Bendern were replaced by new metal ones strong enough to carrying modern traffic.

Construction of a dike on the Liechtenstein side of the Rhine costing 5 million crowns began in 1873. Because the river is narrow there and its fall is slight, a lot of soil and debris gets deposited in its bed between the dikes. Thus the Rhine's riverbed is higher than the surrounding countryside. When the river rises too high and causes a breach, severe flooding results.

The Flood of September 1927 was a disaster. The Rhine became swollen by heavy rainfalls and melting snow in the mountains of the Grisons caused by the Fohn. Sunday morning, September 25, the alarm was raised as whole trees jammed up against the railway bridge near Schaan. Then at 7:00 PM the dam on the Liechtenstein side of the bridge collapsed leaving a hole 300-meter long and destroying the bridge. By the next morning, most of the Lowlands was a lake. Only the roofs of houses stuck out of the floodwaters. Countless trees had been uprooted and cattle washed away to their deaths. The flood reached as far as the village of Mauren.

Appeals went out for help. Switzerland and Austria immediately answered the call sending 235 Swiss firemen and 250 Austrian Alpine troops to help with the rescue work and the repair of the dam. The breach was finally filled in just before Christmas. It was a long time before the fields were dry enough to cultivate. The damage from this terrible flood was estimated at 1.2 million francs.

The steady rising of the Rhine's riverbed is still a problem. The dams have been continuously heightened and the riverbed dredged. Fortunately, in recent years, construction by the Swiss in the Grissons and the removal of a great deal of gravel from the riverbed for road construction has decreased the danger of flooding. Between 1931 and 1943, the Liechtenstein Government built a 30 kilometer canal parallel to the Rhine and joined it to a second one that drains parts of the Underland. Today, you can hike and bike on the dike along the Liechtenstein side of the Rhine and enjoy the beauty of the countryside.

GHOSTS

THE GHOST OF GUTENBURG CASTLE

The Gutenberg Castle in Balzars is said to be haunted by a spirit is of a beautiful white lady who can only be freed from her spell by a young man who can dance around the great hall with her three times without saying a word. If successful, she is free from haunting the castle and the young man will receive a basket full of gold snails. Sometime ago, the locals say, one young man did dance with the ghostly maiden. Just as they were going to complete the third circuit, she touched him with her ice-cold hands causing him to moan out loud. She, of course, then disappeared.

THE GHOST OF SCHELLENBERG CASTLE

The last Werdenberg owner of Schellenberg was a cruel master who was hated by his subjects. While they starved, he and his friends held riotous feasts in the Schellenberg Castle. Then, one night around 1416, when the Count and his cronies were roaring drunk, the oppressed peasants rose up and stormed the castle setting it afire. The Count, escaping on his horse, rode towards the Rhine River where in the stormy darkness he went off a cliff to his death. Now, they say that on dark and stormy nights, his ghost can be seen riding his horse off that same cliff.

THE HOUND OF SANTMERTA

They say that was and may still be a ghost in "Santamerta", the chapel of St. Mamerta in Triesen. One evening a young man was praying there when this ghost materialized and advised him could become rich if he returned with two friends at midnight. A chest of gold would appear but beware as it would be guarded by a hound. He and his friends had to overcome the hound in order to get the gold.

The next midnight, he and his two friends were waiting in the chapel when the chest of gold appeared. But the hound was sitting on it. Two of the men tried to force the hound off the treasure but it would not budge. The third man hung back as he was afraid. Suddenly, the chest of gold and the hound disappeared accompanied by terrible screaming. The ghost materialized again and complained that because of their failure he would have to stay a ghost for another thousand years. Then he disappeared. The three men could not get out of the chapel until the bell for the Angelus prayer was rung by the sacristan in the morning.

DRAGONS

Once upon a time, there were dragons in Liechtenstein. The Rhine Valley was long ago a swamp due to flooding. It appeared sinister to the locals and was said to be the abode of dragons. The mountains and forests were dark and dangerous. Wolves, bears and boars abounded and attacked unwary humans wandering the alpine slopes or stumbling through the festering swamps. Through the ages, the peasants of Liechtenstein worked their fields or herded the cows and sheep in the meadows, albeit with a nervous eye on the wilds surrounding them. When night fell they locked themselves up in stout farmhouses or castle keeps and huddled around their fireplaces and told stories of mysterious and dangerous creatures. Marauding dragons joined the wolves, bears, boars and other terrifying monsters.

In the mountains above Vaduz lie the little hamlets of Gulfina and Silum. A dragon lived in a great cave, near the summit of the range, above the villages and terrorized the local inhabitants. This was a particularly ferocious beast, armored with large thick scales, eyes that glowed like hot coals, huge bat-like wings, a poisonous vapor pouring from its nostrils and a powerful tail. A giant that lived in the mountains finally killed it at the request of the villagers after a terrible battle. The giant was badly hurt but was nursed back to health by one of the local women.

Other dragons were said to live in the nearby mountains of Austria and Switzerland such as the dragon in the cave at Saint-Béat. Christophe Scheurer, a first magistrate of Swiss canton, reported seeing a dragon taking flight from a great rock called Mont Pilate in the early 1700's. He described it as having a body as long as its neck and tail, a head like a toothed serpent and sparks trailing from its body. In the Vorarlberg, a fierce dragon once hunted in the pastures, forests and ravines near Brand. A huge dragon lived in Lake Sonderdach, a small supposedly bottomless lake set in pastures above Bezau while another of its kind guarded a hoard of gold and silver coins under a big rock in Galina Gorge.

Usually, in the west, dragons are thought of as magical creatures created by the devil. As such, they were to be feared and avoided like the Plague. But in the Liechtenstein/Vorarlberg region, they were not thought to be supernatural but just another danger like wolves, bears, and boars. The nobles and knights paid them little attention as they thought that the dragons were no threat to their towns and castles. Dealing with the creatures was left up to the local peasants.

It is possible that a real creature which many think is now extinct could be the basis for the dragons in Liechtenstein and elsewhere in the Alps. It is the Tazelwurm.

Dragons exist no longer in Liechtenstein. Their caves lie empty. But recently a dragon of sorts has returned to the land – a Dragon Boat that is, sponsored by the LGT Bank in Liechtenstein. It took part nearly every year in the Stanley Dragon Boat races in Hong Kong.

THE DRAGON HOLES

On the mountainside behind the villages of Balzars and Mals, are several caves, which the local citizens call the Dragon Holes. Legend says that a fierce dragon lived there over three hundred years ago. Not satisfied with just eating the villagers' livestock, the creature hunted people. When the locals tried to catch him with huge nets, the dragon simply broke loose. As a last resort, his victims appealed to the Virgin Mary for help and promised to build her a church on the spot where the monster ate his prey. The villagers kept them word when their tormentor up and disappeared, never to be seen again. Today, in commemoration of this event, you can visit the small white chapel of the Church of Mariahilf. On its roof is a weathervane in the shape of a dragon.

NOW

ROBBERS, BARONS and KNIGHTS

In Public domain as per http://commons.wikimedia.org/wiki/File:Arthur-Pyle_Mounted_Knight.JPG

Liechtenstein 499 to 843 AD

The people of the Liechtenstein valley were to experience much war and devastation during the Middle Ages. But their strength of character and perseverance would win through and eventually history's twists and turns would lead them into their own nationhood and a time of increasing peace and prosperity. But for the years from the 6th to the 17th century, they would be ruled by a collection of dukes, barons and knight, most of who were greedy, inept and tyrannical.

As Roman power declined in the 5th century, the Alemanni moved into the area. For awhile, both cultures existed side by side. In 496 AD, The Franks under Clovis conquered the Alemanni, and Rhaetia including the Liechtenstein valley became part of the Kingdom of the Franks. Rhaetia had been divided into two parts with the Liechtenstein valley lying in Lower Rhaetia under an Imperial Governor at Curia Rhaetorum (Chur). In 536 AD, the Ostrogoths gained Rhaetia from the Franks and the province became part of the Alemannic Duchy in lower Rhaetia. For many years, members of the Merovigian and Carolingian dynasties, with the help of the Victoriden, a noble family would rule the area. In the 7th Century, the Franks strove to gain control over the Alemanni. The concept of counties was introduced and a Count ruled each county but in answer to the king. At first, under a strong king, this system flourished. Later under corrupt and weak Merovingian rulers, feuds and warfare between Counts of various counties laid waste to the countryside.

In 751 AD, Pipin the Small became the King of the Franks, disposing Childeric III, the last of the Merovingian kings. The Carolingian dynasty was to see great changes in Rhaetia and the valley. In 800 AD, Charlemagne, Pippin's son, was crowned Emperor of the West and King of the Franks. He concentrated all government functions in his hands and pushed the idea of divine right of kings to rule. During his reign, the lands were ruled well and the people prospered. The Christian Church grew strong and gained converts. In 806 AD, Charlemagne gave the Duchy of Chur, which included the Liechtenstein valley at that time, to his son Pippin. In 843, the treaty of Verdun gave the Duchy to Louis the German and it then became part of the

Duchy of Swabia. After nearly three centuries of Frankish rule, Alemannia and Chur-Rhaetia were now under German control.

The Christian Church became the dominant church but vestiges of pagan beliefs still lingered in the valley. The peasants went about their daily lives, raising their families, herding their cattle, fishing and hunting. They paid their taxes and rendered the required services to the local lords and knights as well as to the king. They were the first to suffer in the constant warfare. They lost their homes when the Rhine flooded in the spring. They buried their dead when plagues struck their communities. But the common folk persevered and built the groundwork for the future nation of Liechtenstein.

After 843 AD, the valley that was to become Liechtenstein was owned by a succession of different medieval rulers. After the surrounding region became an earldom under Charlemagne, it was continually divided up among his descendants. It can be a bit confusing as the area was divided, then subdivided and then changed owners all most on whim. Our knowledge about that era is like a puzzle with a few pieces missing. Lets see if we can put most of the puzzle together.

When the last Carolinian emperor died in 911 AD, Retia and Swabis were joined to form the Alemanic Duchy of Chur-Rhaetia. In 1079, the Duchy of Swabia, owned by the house of Hohenstauffen, absorbed the old Chur-Rhaetia Duchy.

In the 12th century, Count Hugo of Montfort succeeded the Counts of Bregenz. As well as the country of Monfort, centered in Feldkirch, he also owned the counties of Werdenberg and Sargans, which included the Liechtenstein valley. Rudolph I inherited Werdenburg and Sargans from his father, Hugo and called himself the Count of Werdenberg.

The keep and the buildings on the east side Vaduz Castle were constructed in the 12th century. The tower is approximately 36 ft. by 39 ft. The ground floor walls are 12 ft. thick in places. An old entrance 33-ft. high was originally on the courtyard side of the structure.

Before 1194, the Knights of Limpach owned Bendern and other estates on the Escherberg when Rudiger von Limpach bequeathed them to the Church of St. Lugi at Chur.

Years before, the Bishops of Chur gained land and influence in the region. In the beginning of the 13th century their power began to diminished. The land that was to become the present principality came under the rule of the Counts of Bregenz in Lower Raetia around 1208.

Also during the 13th century, Hans Varnbueler of Greiffenberg and Gutenberg lived in Gutenberg, the castle at present day Balzars. Around 1250 AD, Schellenberg was acquired by the Barons of Schelleberg. With the passing of the house of Hohenstauffen in 1268 AD, the Duchy of Swabia disintegrated into small lordships, among which were the County of Vaduz and the Lordship of Schellenberg.

Around 1300, the Barons of Frauenberg, of whom minnesinger Heinrich von Frauenberg was well-known, lorded it at Gutenberg Castle in Balzers. Then in

1308, when the Emperor Albrecht von Aar was assassinated the Archdukes of Austria captured the Gutenberg. The owners, thought to be in on the plot were persecuted, and the castle was given to the masters of Ramschwag.

Before 1342, Vaduz was just a small part of the holdings of the Counts of Werdenberg-Sargans. Then, on May 3, 1342 it was made a separate County, and parceled out as part of the Counts of Werdenberg inheritance. Herman of Werdenberg, also known as Graf Hartmann Von Montfort, acquired all the land east of the Rhine when he signed a treaty with his brother, Rudolf IV. He became the first Count of Vaduz to reside in Vaduz Castle.

In 1396, The Emperor Wenzel bestowed Imperial Immediacy on the county of Vaduz, making it a fief of the empire and confirmed the ownership of the Hartman I's son. From this declaration the eventual state of Liechtenstein was to develop.

Thus by the 14th century, the counties of Schellenberg and Vaduz gained their present shape. Four respected families ruled the two counties in turn until the House of Liechtenstein, today's present rulers, purchased them.

THE COUNTS OF WERDENBERG-VADUZ

The old province of Lower Raetia, in the Duchy of Swabia, was at first under the rule of the Counts of Monfort. Around 1200 AD, Hugo of Monfort inherited the family lands, which included the neighboring counties of Werdenberg, Sargans and Feldkirch as well as most of present day Liechtenstein.

If there ever was a ruler who personified the movie cliché "Robber Baron", it was Count Hugo! From his stronghold in Feldkirch, just across the north border of Liechtenstein in Austria, he terrorized the countryside. He robbed passing merchants and travelers and sacked monasteries. His wild ways and avarice frightened his neighbors whom he held in servitude to his whims. For many years, he robbed both the rich and the poor without a thought to his eventual reckoning. Then, when an old man, he decided to hedge his bets by repenting just a little. Did he repent his evil ways? Did he give his fortune to the poor? No, Hugo built a hospital in Feldkirch.

In the 13th century, the lands now comprising the County of Schellenberg was given to the Knights of Schellenberg by the German Emperor of the House of Hohenstaufen. They guarded the approach to the passes of the Alps that were the lines of communication between the Emperor's Swabian and Italian possessions. Later the Lords of Schellenberg transferred their allegiance to the Habsburg emperors. Through skillful service, the Schellenburgers obtained wealth and power. For nearly a hundred years, they were among the favorites at the Imperial court. However, by 1317, their circumstance had deteriorated and they sold the County of Schellenberg for debts to the Counts of Werdenberg. Then the Monfort family split into two different lines of descent – the Monforts and the Werdenbergs. For the next hundred years various descendants of Hugo ruled the land. In its turn, the Werdenberg part of the family further sub-divided into different branches. In 1342, the vast family estates were divided between two brothers. One, named Hartmann of Werdenberg-Sargans, inherited the County of Vaduz, which had just been created as part of the partitioning. Taking up residence in Vaduz Castle, he called himself Count of Vaduz.

In 1379 Count Heinrich of Werdenberg-Vaduz received jurisdiction from the Emperor, King Wenzel. Then in 1396, King Wenzel made the son of Count Heinrich estates a Reichsler or Fief of the Empire, with the right of self-governing. Thus the County of Vaduz were no longer under the sovereignty of the Dukes of Swabia. In the following years, the Emperor reaffirmed the Counts of Vaduz's rights many times.

The Monfort-Werdenberg family ruled the area for two hundred years. But they could not stop entangling themselves in local civil wars and quarreling among themselves. In particular, the Bishops of Chur and the Abbots of St. Gallens, even though related, fought each other over the slightest thing. The Counts of Vaduz feuded with the Feldkirch branch of the family and with the farmers "League of Above the Lake" (Bund ob dem See) from 1405 – 1408. Soldiers of the League occupied Schellenberg during one of these disputes. In the Appenzell War of 1405, the two counties were plundered and pillaged as a monastic army from the Abbey of St. Gall and Austria fighting the army from the free town of St Gall and its allies.

The last Werdenberg owner of Schellenberg was a cruel master who was hated by his subjects. While they starved, he and his friends held riotous feasts in the Schellenberg Castle. Then one night around 1416, when the Count and his cronies were roaring drunk, the oppressed peasants rose up and storm the castle setting it afire. The Count, escaping on his horse, rode towards the Rhine River where in the stormy darkness he went off a cliff to his death.

By 1416 AD the Monfort-Werdenberg family had lost their fortune and, in order to pay their debts, pledged the County of Vaduz to the Brandis family. The Barons of Brandis quickly took possession of Vaduz. Baron Wolhhard of Brandis then brought the County of Schellenberg from the remaining relatives of the dead Count of Werdenberg. Now the greater part of the Liechtenstein valley was united under one ruler.

BARON VON BRANDIS

The family von Brandis brought the county of Vaduz in 1416 and Schellenberg in 1419. Originally from Switzerland, they were related by marriage with the Werdenbergers - the Counts of Vaduz. When Baron Wolfhard von Brandis, the head of the family, took possession of his new domains, the Old World was changing and new ways were taking root. The darkness of the Middle Ages was being replaced by yearnings for religious and personal freedom. The people's imaginations were stirred by discoveries of new lands, inventions and ideas. With change came restlessness. The ordinary people also sought change, many rising up against their oppressors.

In the Baron's new lands, the old and new castles at Schellenberg had been burnt by vengeful peasants. The von Brandis was smart enough to give the people some of what they wanted while keeping most of the power in their own hands. These concessions became known as the "Brandis Freedoms". All men able to bear arms were given the right to elect their own village councilors for a moot or special gathering where they could air their grievances.

By 1434, Schellenberg had reached its present boundaries and the two counties were united under one ruler. In 1441, when the Swiss Federation went to war against the Dukes of Austria, Baron Brandis, angry with the Swiss interference in his business, sided with the Dukes. Sporadic fighting and squabbling went on for years with each side harassing the other. Spies and troublemakers were dispatch to each other's territories. A Swiss spy, who tried to set fires in Feldkirch, was caught and burned at the stake.

During the War of Succession of the Toggenbugers, Baron Wolfhard, fighting for the Austrians, lost the battle of Ragnaz in 1446. The Swiss, in retaliation, captured the villages of Balzers and Triesen.

The Barons of Brandiz seemed to always get themselves embroiled in their neighbor's affairs and wars. In 1499, the Baron sided with the Swabian and Imperial Austrian against the Swiss. It turned out to be a diaster. In early 1499, a peace was agreed on at Feldkirch but did not last long. The Austrian garrison in Castle Gutenberg ridiculed passing Swiss troops, who took offence. The Swiss burnt down a nearby house. The conflict escalated into a battle that left a hundred dead. Then the Swiss again invaded the Brandis lands and captured Vaduz.

Ludwig, the Baron at the time, was apparently not much of a warrior. Hold up in the Castle on the heights over the village of Vaduz, he could have easily held off the invaders with the few troops he had. Instead, he let the Swiss march into the castle unopposed and even tried to bribe them to leave him alone. This strategy did not work. The Swiss army looted the castle, setting it on fire and took the Baron as a prisoner. The surrounding villages were also looted and the inhabitants forced to swear allegiance to the Swiss

Confederation. Baron Ludwig was carried off into Switzerland where it took his lawyers nine months to secure his freedom and the return of his lands.

Several weeks later, the Swiss crossed the Rhine at Schaan in order to attack the Austrians at Feldkirch. The local inhabitants fled into the mountains to escape the advancing army. A traitor showed the Swiss the way to a mountain ridge above Planken and Gafadura, from where they could surprise their unsuspecting enemies. Alas, instead of receiving money, the traitor had his head removed by the Swiss. The Swiss attacked and drove the Austrian army back on Feldkirch. The castle of Gutenberg held out against all the Swiss threw at them. The Swiss' guns had no effect against the stout walls of Gutenberg Castle. A story is told of how the maids in the castle would get up on the ramparts each morning and with brooms sweep off the walls the marks left by swiss cannon balls. A huge gun made by a famous gun maker from France blew up the first time it was fired. The troubles dragged on until peace was restored on September 12, 1499.

When Baron Ludwig von Brandis returned to his home, his troubles were still not over. He had no money left to pay his lawyers. He passed away before he could settle his debts. In 1507, to pay off the family's debts, Vaduz and Schellenberg were sold to Count Rudolf von Sulz, Ludwig's nephew from Swabia.

For awhile, the people of Vaduz and Schellenberg, under the Sulzs, were to enjoy relative peace while all around them, the Reformation and Counter-reformation surged. They remained Catholic while their neighbors embraced the new Protestant religion. But even the peace proved to be tenuous.

THE COUNTS OF SULZ - A CENTURY OF PEACE

When Count Rudolf von Sulz bought Vaduz and Schellenberg in 1507, the Liechtenstein area came under Hapburgs and German control and was no longer dominated by the Swiss and Rhaetians. Under the rule of the Sulz family, the people of the Liechtenstein valley were to enjoy a century of peace.

The Counts of Sulz ruled the two small dominions from their seat in Klettgau (Baden). One of the first things Count Rudolph did was to rebuild Vaduz castle and fortify it with cannons. In 1528, 1531 and 1543, Count Rudolf built two round towers on the north and south side of Castle Vaduz and added the western wall that looks out over the valley. He also instituted a warning system where gunshots from the castles of Gutenberg, Bendern and Vaduz would warn the populace of impending attack. All the able-bodied men would then arm themselves and gather at Rankweil ready for battle.

The rights of the people were also improved. The Sulz established a court-municipality in each county. The local citizens appointed a president and twelve judges to represent them. The courts (the so-called time court or "Zeitgericht") convened twice a year. These rights were to last down to the present time and formed part of the foundation of the present state of Liechtenstein. He also abolished the old custom requiring all serfs to leave part of their property to their lord when they died and lowered the compulsory labors days to three in a year.

The Sulz were also able to keep their domains out of local disastrous wars and well as the on-going religious conflicts. They were Catholics and were able to persuade their charges to remain Catholic during the turmoil of the Reformation. Across the Rhine in Switzerland, the Protestant cause gained ground, especially with Zwingli (the great Swiss Reformer) preaching in his home at Wilhaus only 20 kilomteres from the border.

There was some excitement in 1553 when the Turks were threatening to invade Central Europe. The Sulz collected a special "Turkish Tax" to help fight the war. According to the records, seventy subjects in Schaan and Planken and fifty in Vaduz had to pay this special tax.

However, there was a hard side to the Sulz rule. The teaching of Protestantism was strictly forbidden and its followers were exiled from the counties. The subjects of Sulz were forbidden to marry Protestants. In 1590, Count Karl-Ludwig proclaimed new laws governing usury and extravagance as well as requiring his loyal Catholic subjects to attend mass on Sundays and holidays and evening prayers. He also came out against swearing, wasting time in the local inns sitting about, playing cards, adultery, over indulging in food and clothing and general all around laziness. He told his subjects how to raise their children. Thus it might be said that the Sulz ruled Vaduz and Schellenberg with and iron hand in a velvet glove.

Despite the stern rule, Count Karl-Ludwig was very popular with his people in Vaduz and Schellenberg. When they heard that he was going to sell the counties, they offered him large sums of money to stay as their Lord. He, however, declined their offer.

Through a combination of political acumen and benevolent but stern rule, the Sulz were able to spare the inhabitants of Vaduz and Schellenberg the horrors of war and religious controversy for over one hundred years. The Sulz years might even be looked back on as a "golden age." In fact, the family was known as the "lucky Sulz."

But even that peaceful time did not last. Poor finances forced Ludwig, the last of the Sulz, to sell his two domains in 1613 to his son-in-law, Count Kaspar of Hohenems. The Earls of Hohenems were at the zenith of their power and wanted to use the Counties of Vaduz and Schellenberg as part of a buffer state between Austria and Switzerland. The people of Liechtenstein were to experience yet another period of war, invasion, devastation, epidemics, plague and witch hunts with the disintegration of the Holy Roman Empire and the Thirty Years War.

THE HOHEMEMS

When Ludwig, the last of the Counts of Sulz, sold Vaduz and Schellenburg to his son-in-law, Count Kaspar of Hohenems, the people of Liechtenstein were to experience a century of war, pestilence, famine and evil. By 1613, France had cut off the communications routes from Italy to Burgundy and Flanders, forcing the Spanish to use the passes of the Central Alps in the Habsburg territories in Italy and Tyrol. This route used the Splugen Road that ran down the east side of the Rhine River in the Liechtenstein Valley. Across the river on the west side was the Protestants of Grisons in the Engadin, the Pratigau (the Landquart valley) and Chur who were allies of France. They controlled the road between the Lusiensteig and Splugen. Thus the stage was set for a steady stream of invasions, famines and epidemics.

The Counts of Hohenems were at the zenith of their power and as allies of the Austrians wanted to set up a buffer state between Austria and Switzerland. They paid taxes to both the Holy Roman Empire and the Swabian League. In 1614, the subjects of Count Kaspar complained vehemently about the high rate of taxation. After some discussion, they came to a mutual agreement. This argument was a prelude to the Thirty Years War. In 1618, the disagreements between Catholics and Protestants broke out into war. The fighting raged sporadically in various places between different groups and countries. Austrian troops occupied the Luziensteig in 1620. In the following year Graubunden and Austria went to war against each other. Even though the two counties took no part, they were not spared. Both sides sent troops though the valley, looting and plundering the inhabitants. The misery and poverty caused by the fighting continued after a peace treaty was signed in 1622. Crops failed, bread became scarce and there was no wine left for the people to down their sorrows in. To make matters worse, that same year, the people of the Pratigau rebelled against the Austrian Emperor. They captured the Luziensteig, and plundered all the villages of Vaduz County before they were defeated near Feldkirch.

Then it got even worse. The Black Plague broke out around 1634 sweeping Europe and killing thousands. Many of the inhabitants of the valley fled into the mountains in the vain hope of escaping the contagion. War continued to surge back and forth over the region. Finally the counties of Vaduz and Schellenberg were forced to join the war on the Austrian side in order to survive. More misfortune was to befall the two counties. In 1647 The Swedes under Wallenstin broke into the valley despite a heroic defense by the local militia and extorted money from the inhabitants before destroying anything not already destroyed in thirty years of constant war. The year, 1648, brought peace but at a terrible price. The inhabitants of Vaduz and Schellenberg were destitute and starving. One seventh of the population perished during these years of turmoil and famine. Nothing remained but empty houses and staving villagers. The morals and manners of the people declined. Local priests complained to the government who passed strict laws against the sinful ways of their subjects. But the misery continued.

Ignoring the poverty and misery around him, Count Franz Maria of Hohenems lived in great extravagance and waste. In 1642, he got married in an elaborate and expensive ceremony in Vaduz Castle. Even while the Thirty Years War devastated the valley, he spent money wrung from his starving subjects to beautify the castle. Luckily for his oppressed subjects, he died several months later.

A different plague now scoured the valley. Witch hunting added to the horror and misery of the people. Fueled by fear, ignorance and greed and ambition, men, women and children denounced family, friends and complete stranger to the authorities. Innocent people were tortured until they confessed, then beheaded or burnt at the stake. Whole families perished. In August of 1648, fourteen victims were put to death in Vaduz alone. In the end over three hundred out of a population of three thousand fell victim to the witch hunting terror, before it was finally stopped by the authorities.

Franz Wilhelm, Count of Vaduz from 1646-1662, followed in his family tradition. He spent more money than he had and then heavily taxed the inhabitants of his county to pay his debts. His son was even more disliked as he continued his father's ways and greatly increased the family debts. He even refused to help his brothers and sisters forcing them to live in relative poverty. Higher authorities shrugged off the people complaints.

Finally, the Emperor could not ignore the situation any longer. First he removed Count Jacob Hannibal, who had acceded Franz Wilhelm's son and appointed an imperial official to sell his estates to pay the family debts. Prince Johann Adam of the House of Liechtenstein brought the County of Schellenberg in 1692 and then Vaduz in 1712. It is from these two dates that the modern history of the Principality of Liechtenstein begins.

ACHIEVING THE IMPERIAL DREAM

In 1707, the counties of Schellenberg and Vaduz were under the control of the Swabian League which was in financial difficulty. On November 25, 1707 Prince Hans Adam came to its rescue with a loan of 250,000 guilders. As a reward he was given a seat on the Council of the Swabian League. But it was a hollow gain as the position was "ad personam" with no real authority or influence. The League paid 75,000 guilders in 1737. Later on Feb. 2, 1809, the Prince of Liechtenstein, the Kings of Bavaria and of Wurtemberg, the Grand-Duke of Hesse reached an agreement on the repayment of the remaining sum owed the Prince.

Count Jacob Hannibal of Hohenems could still not pay his debts and his property was put up for sale to cover what he owed. On February 22, 1712,

Prince Johann Adam von und zu Liechtenstein bought the county of Vaduz for 290,000 Gulden. This with the county of Schellenberg gave him a seat and a vote in the Imperial government.

On June 16, 1712, Prince Hans Adam died. He is remembered because of his achievements, especially adding the precious stone of the Principality of Liechtenstein to his family's crown.

As Prince Hans Adam had no sons when he died, his great-nephew Aton Florian (1656-1721) should have become the reigning Prince. The Prince's will, however, stated that Prince Wenzel (1696-1772) was to inherit the counties of Vaduz and Schellenberg. There were protracted negotiations between the two aspiring princes, which was not settled until 1718. In the meantime, Prince Wenzel ruled the two counties. His agent, a man called Harprecht, administered the area and seemed to care little for the inhabitants. He worked ceaselessly to erode the functions of the "Landammaner" and increase the authority and fortune of the Prince at the expense of the people.
On March 12, 1718, the Emperor sanctioned an agreement to an exchange by the two princes. Aton Florian became Prince of Liechtenstein and ruler of Vaduz and Schellenberg while Josef Wenzel got the large county of Rumburg and the promissory notes for the 250,000 guilders loaned to the Swabian League. Wenzel however would rule the little country again in 1748.

Once more, the people of the counties of Vaduz and Schellenberg gather to swear allegiance to a new ruler. On September 5, 1718, they swore the oath of allegiance before the Prince's detested emissary, Harprecht, in Vaduz. A new coat of arms and colors replaced the old ones in Vaduz Castle.

Then, on January 23, 1719, Kaiser Karl VI made the counties of Vaduz and Schellenberg into a principality with the name Liechtenstein in honor of his loyal servant Anton Florian of Liechtenstein. The new Principality of Liechtenstein was the 343rd of the Holy Roman Empire. As the ruler of the little principality, not yet a country, the Prince owed allegiance directly to the Emperor and contributed financially and militarily to the support of the Imperial Crown.

Prince Anton Florian gained a powerful seat on the Imperial Diet. The goal, that four generations of the house of Liechtenstein had been striving for, had been reached. For over a hundred years the rulers of this little land stayed in Vienna, the seat of Imperial power and ignored their subjects. Succeeding Princes left the administration and care of the two counties in the hands of administrators or commissioners such as Cristoph Harprecht. This circumstance led to a struggle between the absolute monarchy of the Prince and the ancient rights of his subjects but that is another story to be told at another time.

WAR AND VICTORY

Painted by Captⁿ. W McKenzie BATTLE OF CULLODEN. In public domain as per
http://www.gutenberg.org/files/25879/25879-h/25879-h.htm

ROMAN LIECHTENSTEIN

By 15 BC, the Romans had pushed north under Tiberius and Drusus, stepsons of Emperor Augustus over the Alps. Their army defeated the Rhaetians and Rhaetia became a Roman province named of course Rhaetia. It included parts of south Bavaria, Vorarlberg, Tyrol and eastern Switzerland covering the territory between Verona in Italy and Lake Constance in Switzerland. The Liechtenstein Valley as part of this area came under Roman control. But further to the north and east were the Germanic tribes that had been steadily moving westward, killing the local inhabitants or driving them before them.

The Romans built a road, the Splugen, from the south over the Mountain passes to the north. In the Liechtenstein valley, it ran along the east bank of the Rhine. Roman Villas and fortifications were built at present day Schaanwald and Nendeln to protect the road across the alpine passes from attack. After the Alamans defeated the Romans in the Teutoburger Forest in 9 AD, Rome did not try to expand any further across the Rhine for a time. To protect Roman colonies in Rhaetia, the Legions built and garrisoned a series of fortifications called Limes.

The Limes to the north and east in the Roman province of Germania Superior were a high spiked wooden fence with a ditch or moat. Just behind that was a thick stone wall with high wooden watch towers. Smaller fortifications housing the Auxilia (auxiliary troops), Cohorts (troops), and Alen (mounted troops) were established behind the wall. These troops called out only in case of serious attack by the German tribes. The Limes in Rhaetia was a single stone wall with manned watchtowers.

The inhabitants of the Liechtenstein valley and Rhaetia became quite romanized during the Imperial years. Roman divinities were worshiped instead of the old Celtic Gods. Commerce increased and agriculture flourished. Vineyards were planted on the mountain slopes. Buildings were built with under the floor heating, running water and sewer disposal. Except for the occasional raid, life in the valley must have been peaceful and prosperous. The Romans would have the least impact on this little country leaving only several ruins. The next group of invaders, The Alamani, would leave their genetic and cultural stamp on the people of Liechtenstein.

From AD 98-117 Roman legions pushed the "Pax Romana" beyond the Rhine to the Main and Danube Rivers. For a time the Germanic tribes were held at bay. With Roman rule came the first Christians. Little is know of them except that they were initially considered subversive and Roman Governors of Rhaetia tried to suppress them. Gradually Christianity took hold in the valley. It is said that the first Christian missionary was St Lucius who came over the mountains from the south on a trail that is still called the Luziensteig. He is venerated as the first apostle of the faith in Liechtenstein.

The Alamans started to move again, repeatedly attacking the Limes after 233 AD. By 260 AD, they had broken through the fortifications and forced the Romans back to the Rhine, the Bodensee and the Danube. It was only be a matter of time before the Germanic tribes invaded the peaceful valley of Roman Liechtenstein.

Then in 261 AD the Alemanni invaded Rhaetia and rampage down the Splugen road through the Liechtenstein valley chasing Emperor Gallienus. At Milan, Gallerius defeated them and chase them back over the Alps to the Black Forest. The Alemanni returned in 264 AD and started to settle the region north of Liechtenstein while fending off the attacks of the Burgundians. For awhile, the Liechtenstein valley saw relative peace still under Roman rule punctuated with barbarian raids.

In 313 AD, the Emperor Constantine adopted Christianity as official religion of the Roman Empire. Shortly thereafter, a bishopric was established at Chur to the southwest of Liechtenstein. Christianity became more excepted it the Alpine valleys.

The Alemanni along with other Germanic tribes swarmed crossed the frozen Rhine in 406-407 and settled in the northern part of modern Switzerland. The people of the Liechtenstein valley were still left in peace as the Alemanni expanded westward and came into conflict with the Franks. Then came the Huns under Atila who raided far into France before they were defeated.

The Ostrogoths invaded Italy in 488 AD and tried to revive the Roman Empire. Chlodwig, Merovingian Ruler of the Franks, defeated the Alemanni some who sought refuge in the Rhaetian Alps, now part of the Ostrogoths kingdom. In 496 AD, Clovis incorporated the Alemanni into his Frankish dominions. Rhaetia divided into two parts. Upper part stretched from the Lake of Constance to Donau with the lower part consisting of the Alpine region up to Kae of the Constance with its capital at Curia Rhaetorum (Chur).

By 536 AD, a lieutenant of a Frankish king ruled the Alemanni and the inhabitants of the Liechtenstein valley. The modern French word Allemagne - "Germany" comes "Alamannia" as the region became known as. Frankish administration and Christianity supplanted the pagan ways but not entirely. Some vestiges still remain as in Halloween.

The territory of the Alemanni remained a separate administrative area, the Duchy of Alamannia (Swabia). The culture and psyche of the Alemanni became the foundation of the national character of the Liechtenstein people.

In 450 AD, the Huns under their leader, Attila, invaded Western Europe crossing the Rhine. A Gallo-Roman army under the Roman General Aetius defeated them at the battle of Chalons. They rode small ponies and flew the banner of a green cat on a red field. The Huns had crossed the Rhine in the general area of present day Liechtenstein, sweeping through the valley, plundering and killing the inhabitants. The locals buried some their treasures but the invaders soon stripped the countryside of everything they could carry before heading west. Roman coins, buried back then, are still being found today.

THE APPENZELL WAR

Through the centuries, the little land of Liechtenstein has been invaded many times. From the Celts, Romans and Alemanni to the French in the Napoleonic Wars, the people of the two counties of Schellenburg and Vaduz suffered occupation, pillaging, plundering and terror. At times they were even invaded by their neighbors across the Rhine. Even the people of the present Swiss Canton of Appenzell had their turn at conquering and occupying Liechtenstein.

The Monfort-Werdenberg family had ruled the area for two hundred years. But they could not stop entangling themselves in local civil wars and quarreling among themselves. In particular, the Bishops of Chur and the Abbots of St. Gallens, even though related, fought each other over the slightest thing. The Counts of Vaduz feuded with the Feldkirch branch of the family and with the farmers "League of Above the Lake" (Bund ob dem See) from 1405 – 1408.

The Abbot of St. Gallen had his hands full with the proud people of the Appenzell who had many grievances against him. But what really set them off was his move to recognize the Dukes of Austria as his liege lords. With their help, he hoped to put an end once and for all to disturbances in his domain. The people of Appenzell felt that their rights were in danger as well as the safety of the Swiss Confederation if the Dukes extended their power into the area. The Schwytz supported Appenzell, while Zurich favored the Bishop of St. Gallen. The war was on.

A number of states and towns such as Thur valley, St. Gallen, Feldkirch and Bludenz, Appenzell, Rheintal, Glarus, Fussach, Hochst, Rankweil, Walgau, Montafon, and feudal lords like Count Rudolph of Werdenberg, formed a confederation called the Bund ob dem Bodensee.

At Voegelinsegg on 15 May, 1403, the men of Appenzell defeated the combined armies of the Bishop of St. Gallen and his Swabian allies. This did not stop the plundering and pillage of the two counties by a monastic army from the Abbey of St. Gallen and Austria. The men of Appenzell then defeated the Abbot and Frederick IV of Austria, at Stoss on 17 June, 1405. Soldiers of the League occupied Schellenberg and the people of the County of Schellenberg were forced to swear allegiance to the Appenzell League. The upper and lower Schellenberg castles were pulled down and burnt.

The League's fortunes did not last long. With the defeat of the Appenzell army at Bregenz on 13 January 1408, the League fell apart. The Swiss Confederation signed a treaty with Appenzell on 24 November, 1408 and with St Gallen on 14 December, 1412 effectively ending the hostilities. The county of Schellenberg reverted back to its previous owner.

The memories of these times linger even today on both sides of the border. It is said that the Apppenzellers, noted for their stubborn nature and long memories, feel that they still have a territorial claim to the two counties.

WAR OF THE SECOND COALITION

In 1798, the Helvetian Republic was formed under French guidance in Switzerland. A French Alliance with the new republic on 19 August, 1798 encouraged the Helvetians to annex Graubünden, just across the Austrian border south and west of Liechtenstein and also the Vorarlberg. The Austrians, of course, were a bit upset and began to strengthen their defenses. They formed new alliances and built up their armies. They also tried to suppress any revolutionary ideas.

Baron Franz von Auffenberg, the commanding general of the Austrian military in Vorarlberg, had recommended that miltia units be formed. On August 9, 1798, Vorarlberg's leaders formed two militia units totaling 3,000 men.

On Dec. 24, 1798, Austria, Great Britain, Russia, Turkey, Naples, Portugal and the Vatican formed the Second Coalition against the French. The French countered by moving several armies to their eastern borders. This border ran roughly along the Rhine River. The Principality of Liechtenstein sat squarely on the front lines of the impending conflict. The French stationed an army of 40,000 men under Marshal Jourdan in the Lake Constance and Schaffhausen region. Another 30,000 troops were with Marshals Massena and Oudinot in Eastern Switzerland. To oppose Massena, the Austrians stationed their armies in the Vorarlland and Grisons, 13,000 men under Von Hotze at Berenz, 7000 troops under Auffenberg near Chur, 5000 at Feldkirch, and two Austrian battalions totaling a 1000 men with four cannons on the Luziensteig near Mayenfeld. The Austrian has also been working frantically on their fortifications in Vorlaberg as well as stocking large warehouses in Feldkirch and Bregenz with necessary supplies to fight a war.

In January of 1799, Vorarlberg with a population of around 85,000 had raised a force of 10,000 men. The mixture of career soldiers, militiamen and locals were whipped into a fighting force. The troops from the Feldkirch area were commanded by a local Captain Alfons von Gerbert. There was also six battalions of regular soldiers consisting of Austrian line infantry and troops from the Croatian border, numbering nearly 3,000 men. Every male between the ages of 16 and 60 were called up to help defend the area. They armed themselves with what ever weapon they could find.

The Coalition planned to begin operations in April 1799 with 125,000 men in Southern Germany, 60,000 in western Austria and 110,000 Russians under the famous Field Marshall Alexander Suvorov in Italy. Baron Friedrich von Hotze with a corps of anti-French Swiss soldiers stood guard along the Rhine in Vorarlberg, Liechtenstein and the Swiss border areas of Luziensteig and Graubünden.

The French with 200,000 men in five armies planned to strike in the beginning of March of 1799 but on hearing of the Russian movement in Italy attacked in the Upper Rhine to prevent the Austrians and Russians from linking up.

Feldkirch was chosen as the place where the Austrian made their main defense. It sat on the strategic crossroads in the Central Alps. Here lay the Rhine Valley and the road from the Arlberg, and the mountain range east of Feldkirch. To the west lay Switzerland. The Ill River with the main bridge, then the Heiligkreuzbrücke, the Holy Cross Bridge, joins the Rhine at this point. Invaders found the surrounding mountains as natural barrier to their easy approach to the city. To the north lay the Ardetzenberg, to the west the Schellenberg and the Blasenberg while to the east were the Stadtschrofen and the Känzele and the towering cliffs of the Ill River Gorge. The weakest point in Feldkirch's defenses was the valley to the south - Liechtenstein. The Austrians built two lines of strong fortifications between the city and the little Principality. The old fortifications such as Castle Schattenberg, built in the middle ages, had lost their defensive value as the city had spread a ways beyond them.

THE BATTLE OF FELDKIRCH MARCH 1799 AND THE FRENCH OCCUPATION

On March 4, 1799, the Austrians called up the Vorarlberg militia. They took their positions ready to repulse the French advance. A small troop was stationed in the Vaduz castle on the hill above the village.

The Directory - Napoleon was not yet Emperor - ordered the two Marshals to take the offensive early in 1799. In the first week of March, 1799, the French under Messena crossed the Rhine near Bendern heading north to the Eschnerberg just south of Feldkirch. Oudinot stormed the Luziensteig scattering the Austrians in three days of hard fighting. Other French forces crossed the frontier at Strassburg and Basel. By nightfall of March 6th 1799 the French have reached and occupied the Schellenberg. They stationed their cannons on the Gantenstein to fire at the fortifications outside Feldkrirch. The Rhine Valley south in Liechtenstein was in the hands of the French.

On March 7, outnumbered Austrian troops tried to drive the French from their newly won positions, but the attack from four sides failed putting the Austrians on the defensive. The hard-pressed Austrians were only saved by a heavy snowfall that forced the French to seemingly hold up and seek warm dry shelter. Then, around noon, as the Austrian were pulling falling back on Feldkirch, the French attacked their flank taking 675 Croatian troops prisoner. The French attacked again, this time at the Mauser Wiese, a meadow in the Rhine Valley south of Feldkirch, driving the Austrians back and advancing as far as the Letzebühel, a hill just east of the road south to Liechtenstein.

In order to attack Feldkirch from the rear, the French moved towards Frastanz. Three companies of marksmen from the village of Montafon stopped them. A concentrated artillery barrage by the Austrians also stopped a French attack along the main road from Liechtenstein to Tisis. The French had reached the last entrenchment when their field commander, General Mueller, was fatally wounded. They fell back in disarray to the Principality's border and regrouped at their headquarters at Nendeln.

The Austrians took advantage of the lull in battle to strengthen their defenses especially the Letzebühel front, a hill above the Tisis Road to Liechtenstein. They thought that the French would try a two-prong attack, one to the east towards Frastanz by way of the Letzebühel and the other along the

Schellenberg to the Ill River. The Letzebühel was the site of an important battle with the Swiss in 1499 during the Appenzeller War.

On March 9, The Austrian moved troops to cover both their eastern and western fortifications. The French meanwhile drank, caroused and plundered the land under their control including Liechtenstein. They smashed furniture, killed livestock or chopped their feet off and abused the local people. They demanded money and wine from the inhabitants threatening death if they did not get it. Four farmers were shot at Murren while many were wounded. Women were raped. It was reported that they nailed an old man to a barn door in Eschen. Whether the atrocities was true or not, the Austrian defenders, when they heard of them, vowed revenge and declared that no Frenchman would set foot in the Vorarlberg.

The village of Ruggell on the Rhine of the Schellenberg was spared most of the devastation of the Frech occupation but had much food and livestock taken by French troops as well as Austrian and Russian troops later.

On March 11 and 12, the Austrian, pulled some troops out of Feldkirch to stiff their forces on their left flank on the Bodensse. Four battalions were rushed from southern Germany to take their place at Feldkirch.

The front stayed quiet until Good Friday, March 22, when the French started to advance early in the morning towards Feldkirch in the country between Nendeln and Tisis on the Liechtenstein border. A unit of riflemen from Bludenz was sent to hold the village of Mauren while 50 men from the Rankweil rifle company and four companies of Altenstadt militiamen rushed to the Schellenberg. Austrian riflemen from Bludenz and regular Austrian troops in Murren held off the French until 2 PM. when they were forced to retreat to St Antonius on the edge of Feldkirch to prevent being cut off.

The Austrian militiamen defending the Schellenberg held off a force ten times their size. When the French brought two cannon up to shield their position, the little unit of 55 men was redrawn slowly fighting the French step by step, tree by tree. This courageous unit suffered only three militiamen wounded while inflicting greater casualties on the French. The battle continued between Tisis and Nendeln until evening without either side giving further ground. A temporary truce was arranged to give both armies time to lick their wounds.

The decisive battle began on Holy Saturday, March 23. Early in the morning, General Nassena sent his 18,000 French troops forward towards Feldkirch. The Austrians on Blasenberg Hill warn the commanders in the city of the French advance up the Schellenberg. Austrian troops, attending church rushed to their defenses. At the height of the battle, all looked lost as the Austrians began to run out of powder. The French had advanced to the barricades just outside Feldkirch. Then crowds of women rushed up to the walls and barricades and joined the men in defending their homes. They rained a hail of stones, chunks of wood on the French, breaking the attack and forcing the enemy to retreat.

More French troops then moved up and forced the Austrians back to St. Antonius, part of present day Feldkirch suburb of Tisis. A company of the Peterwardeiner Border Battalion halted this advance. A second company counterattacked and ended the French breakthrough. The French under

Massena continued to press their attack up the center on the road from Nendeln to Tisis.

Meanwhile, another French force tried to outflank the Austrians by climbing the steep Hohen Älpele, a mountain above Letze, on the flank of the Letze fortifications. By 4 PM. they had reached the area known as the "Bear Cave". The Austrians sent their last reserve of four companies to the high ground of the Letzebühel. Other militiamen attacked over a nearby ridge and hit the Frecnh in their rear at the Bear Cave forcing the French to retreat. The French tried one more attack which wass stop by a combined barrage of Austrian artillery. The Battle for Feldkirch wass over. The French suffered 2,200 casualties while the Austrians had 96 dead, 590 wounded and 100 taken prisoner.

General Massena withdrew his forces to Graubünden and General Oudinot crossed back over the Rhine. The retreating French devastated the countryside as they retreated.

The Austrians followed the French back down the Liechtenstein side of the Rhine valley and retook the Luziensteig. Archduke Charles crossed the Rhine at Stein while Hotze crossed at Balzers. Between them, they drove Massena back to Zurich. The French occupation of the Principality lasted only three weeks this time.

A Russian Army even invaded Liechtenstein at this time. The Russians were allied with Austria against the French and sent several armies to fight them. Aleksandr Vasilyevich Suvorov commanded the allied forces in northern Italy and beat the French in three battles at Cassano d'Adda, the Trebbia River, and Novi Ligure. Suvorov in October, 1799 led a force of 20,000 men across the Alps to join the Russian forces fighting the French in Switzerland. His march through the Alps against great odds was one of the most fantastic adventures in military history.

Suvorov was forced due to circumstance to retreat from Zurich. The Archduke Charles had abandon Switzerland and Korsakov's army had been completely routed by Massena and Soult at the second Battle of Zurich on September 25th.

A myth has grown up around the Battle of Feldkirch in 1799. According to the "Bells of Retreat", the French under Napoleon had advance within six miles of the Fortress at Feldkirch in Vorarlberg, Austria and were on the verge of taking the city without resistance. As the French approached during the night the people of Feldkirch, all good Catholics, gathered in their churches to pray for deliverance from the French.

The next morning, Easter Sunday, at sunrise the bells rang out over the countryside. The French, not realizing that it was Easter Sunday, thought that the bells were being rung in joy for the arrival of the Austrian army in Feldkirch. Napoleon quickly ordered a retreat and the city was saved!

If this incident occurred in 1799, it could not have been Napoleon in command of the French. He was in Egypt at this time. A battle was fought at Feldkirch in 1799 and the French were defeated. The French had also attacked the city in

1796/97, 1800 and 1805 and occupied the city at these times. The legend of the Bells of Retreat appears to be a case of wishful thinking.

THE 19TH CENTURY 1800-1899

In the Year 1800, the French under Marshal Jourdan once again invaded Liechtenstein from the Grissons. They marched up the east side of the Rhine towards Feldkirch. It would be relatively quiet in leichtenstein until 1865.

THE AUSTRIAN-PRUSSIAN WAR

By the end of 1865, the threat of war once again loamed over the Principality. Bismarck of Prussia was empire building and willing to go to war to achieve his end. The treat subsided somewhat in August of 1865 with the Treaty of Gastein. But Bismarck was still not satisfied and the fate of three duchies of Schleswig, Holstein and Lauenburg was undecided. Then, on April 8, 1866, encouraged by Napoleon III's passive attitude, Bismark arranged an alliance with Italy.

This did not sit well with Austria, Prussia's foe in the German Confederation. It was now had to face two enemies. Bismarck's next move to exclude Austria from the German Confederation enraged Austrians and their allies. Austria then demanded on June 11, 1866, that Diet vote on mobilizing troops against Prussia. On June 14, the Diet voted 9 for mobilization and 7 against.

Bismarck was furious. He blamed little Liechtenstein for the decision. How was the Principality to blame? According to a circular published at that time, the little states in the Confederation had too much representation all out of proportion to their size. The larger and medium sized states had one vote each, while the smaller ones, grouped in Curias, had one vote each. Within the Curias, they decided their stance by a simple majority. The 16th Curia composed of six small states had voted for mobilization. Bismarck's supporters claimed that only Liechtenstein had voted for mobilization and the majority was against it. They further claimed that due to an error the vote of the Curia was changed to be in favor of Mobilization. If the supposedly correct vote had recorded then, there would have been an equal number against as for. And no mobilization would have taken place. Thus, Bismarck claimed that tiny Liechtenstein had somehow brought about the pro-Austrian vote of the Curia.

This was all the excuse Bismarck needed. He claimed that his country was being unjustly attacked. Why should a country with a population of 6,000 and army of only 80 men have such influence? It was ridiculous and the whole Democratic system and structure of the German Confederation was senseless.

Apparently, the notorious 16th Curia vote in favor of mobilization was the correct one. According to a circular by Baron von Kubeck to the representatives of the Foreign Powers at the Diet, Frankfort, July 14, 1866, Lippe and Waldeck voted against mobilization while Liechtenstein and Reuss-Griez voted for it. Reuss-Schliez abstained and Schaumberg-Lippe voted yes provided no instructions to the contrary were received by June 14th. Two hours after the vote Herr von Strauss, the Minister of Schaumburg-Lippe did receive orders to vote for the mobilization. Thus with the vote three for, two against and one abstention, the Confederation declared for mobilization against Prussia. It was war.

Liechtenstein had a standing army of eighty men and a reserve of twenty. There was not much it could do, but it was willing to try. On July 2, 1866, two days before the Battle of Sadowa, the 16th curia informed the Diet that Prince Johann II would send troops but only to defend German territory in the Tyrol. His army would not fight other Germans but would defend German soil against invaders.

Liechtenstein's little army took up defensive positions on the Stilfser Joch to guard against possible attack by the Italians under Garibaldi's men. Feldweibel Andreas Walch and eight men from Ruggell were part of the contingent.

On July 4th, Prussia defeated the pro-Austrian forces. The armistice of Nicholburg was signed on July 22.

Liechtenstein's little army, undefeated but not tested in battle, marched home. On the way home, an Austrian liaison officer joined the contingent. Thus 80 men had left for war but 81 marched into Vaduz for a ceremonial welcome.

Despite his early accusations of Liechtenstein's duplicity, Bismarck forgot all about Liechtenstein. The Principality was not even mentioned in the Treaty of Prague on August 23. The end of the Austro-Prussian War of 1866 brought about the end of the German Confederation. In its place, Prussia established the North German Confederation under Prussian leadership, of course. Austria and its allies, Liechtenstein included, were excluded. Thus Liechtenstein gained freedom of action in its international affairs. The principality was no longer under any obligation to provide troops.

Some fanciful myths have arisen about Liechtenstein and Prussia. It is claimed that Liechtenstein is still at war with Prussia as there was no peace treaty signed between them. As mentioned, the Treaty of Prague did not mention the little country. Years later, it was claimed that Field-Marshal Moltke of Prussia always avoided Liechtenstein whenever he visited the nearby Swiss Resort of Ragaz for his health. He did not want to travel through enemy country. These stories have no historical base as Liechtenstein and Prussia resumed full diplomatic relations in 1867.

HITLER"S NEMESIS

In 1937, a number of local Nazis and sympathizers tried unsuccessfully to take over the opposition party in Liechtenstein's Parliament. But there was very little difference between the two traditional political parties in the Principality except in the personalities of their leaders. Both parties were "big C" Conservative and anti-socialist. When the Nazi failed, they turned to more violent means. On the night April 14, 1938, the small local Nazi party tried to take over the country. That night, they lit swastika-shaped fires lit up in the Liechtenstein mountains a signal to an SS tank column, waiting at Feldkirch just across the border in Austria. In the morning, they seized the bridges over the Rhine to Switzerland. A number of loyal citizens quickly gathered in Vaduz, and armed with sticks quickly persuaded the Nazi traitors that it was not a good idea to mess with their country. Dr Hoop, head of the government lodged a strong protest via the Swiss government in Berne. Meanwhile a priest, a troop of local boy scouts and a small number of unarmed

Liechtenstein border guards faced the SS column at the border. Then for some unknown reason the SS pulled back and headed away from Liechtenstein. It could not have been for fear of the Swiss even though they had signed a treaty to come to the aid of the little country. In any case, the Swiss had plans to blow the bridges if Hitler had invaded the principality. Thus Liechtenstein was saved from Nazi occupation.

LIECHTENSTEIN'S LAST SOLDIER

In 1939 Liechtenstein's last soldier died. He had taken part in the Austro-Prussian War of 1866. Liechtenstein's army was disbanded in 1868 after the dissolution of the German Confederation. Since then, the little country has had no armed forces except for a police force. However, the constitution allows, that in the events of hostilities, every able-bodied man up to the age of 60 is liable for military service for the defense of the country. Since 1868 Liechtenstein has followed the path of peace and neutrality and not war.

Individual citizens have joined other armies at times. Some enlisted in the Austrian Army and members of the Liechtenstein ruling family served in the Austrian Armed forces over the centuries. A few pro-Nazi Liechtensteiners joined the German Army during World War II after loyal citizens stopped their attempted takeover in 1938. On the whole, the citizens of this little Principality have supported their government in its attempts to remain neutral and avoid war.

But when they had to fight, the citizens of Liechtenstein stood up and fought for what they believed in. In past centuries, whenever they were invaded, the common people fought as a militia. It was not until the Principality of

Liechtenstein was created in 1719 that a regular army was created. Because of the size of the country and small population, the army was never big. The army did, however, see some action. Until the 20th Century, the Austrian army largely looked after the defense of the country. When Liechtenstein aligned itself with Switzerland after World War I, the Swiss Army took over this duty.

In 1789, when the French occupied the Switzerland side of the Rhine, Liechtenstein sent 15 infantrymen and two cavalrymen to serve with the Swabian League. In 1793 a reinforcement of eight men joined Liechtenstein's contingent with the League. A militia, in which all able-bodied men from the age of 18 to 50 had to serve, was also formed for defense. In 1796 Marshal Jourdan marched his French army through the Rhine Valley and forced the Swabian league to surrendered. Liechtenstein was no longer at war. But in 1799 the French again marched through the valley on the way to fight the Austrians and Russians. Napoleon formed the Confederation of the Rhine on July 12, 1806, Liechtenstein was admitted as a member. Prince Johann, in order to fight for Austria, gave up his throne to his young son. After Napoleon's defeat in Russia, the Confederation of the Rhine broke up and Prince Johann regained his throne. Liechtenstein then sent 100 men to fight Napoleon in the army of Baden in 1815.

In 1815, the Congress of Vienna formed a new Confederation of German States and upheld Liechtenstein's sovereignty. A severe famine in 1817 made it impossible for Liechtenstein to meet its military obligations with the German League and the people demanded to be relieved of the cost of the army. The Prince agreed to assume the financing of the small 80-man army.

While citizens were still required to serve in the army, there were occasions when the Prince hired contingents from other countries to take the place of the regular Liechtenstein Army.

Liechtenstein's army, as part of the 8th Army corps, fought in the suppression of in the Baden uprising in 1849.

During the Austro-Prussian War of 1866, Prince Johann II placed his soldiers at the disposal of the Confederation but only to "defend the German territory of Tyrol". The Prince refused to have his men fight against other Germans. The Liechtenstein contingent took up position on the Stilfse Joch in the south of Liechtenstein to defend the Liechtenstein/Austrian border against attacks by the Italians under Garibaldi. A reserve of 20 men remained in Liechtenstein. When the war ended on July 22, the army of Liechtenstein marched home to a ceremonial welcome in Vaduz. Popular legend claims that 80 men went to war but 81 came back. Apparently an Austrian liaison officer joined up with the contingent on the way back.

With dissolving of the German Confederation at the end of the war, the Prince no longer had to provide troops. In 1868, he disband his small army to save money. Liechtenstein then looked to Austria for support in foreign relations until 1918.

The Principality tried to remain neutral especially in World War One and Two. Because of its close relationship to Austria during the First World War, the victorious Allies treated it as a co-belligerent. Though suffering much hardship, the people of Liechtenstein persevered in their quest for neutrality and peace.

With the passing of Liechtenstein's last soldier in 1939, the last vestiges of Liechtenstein's army disappeared. Today, the Principality walks the road of peace and welcomes more refugees per capita than any other nation. Liechtenstein no longer uses war as a tool to further its political aspiration and ends. Perhaps other bigger nations could take a lesson from this small country.

STALIN'S NEMISIS

As the war in Europe can to an end in the spring of 1945, Liechtenstein once again displayed its resolve and independence. On the evening of May 2, 1945, another army approached the borders of Liechtenstein near Schellenberg. This time they were not trying to invade but to seek asylum. The column of White Russian Soldiers under the command of Major-General Count A. Holmston-Smyslowsky had fought for Germany against the Communists in Russia. With them came many women and children.

The local commander of the Frontier Police having heard of the military column gathered what men he could. As he and his small force drove up the road from Schellenberg towards the border near the Austrian city of Feldkirch, lines of armed soldiers flying the white, blue and red flag of Imperial Russia appeared ahead on either side of the road. On the road itself a column of cars and trucks approached slowly. The Liechtenstein police officer ordered the column to stop. When it failed to do so, he ordered his outnumbered and out gunned men to fire warning shots. The Russians did not fire back. A stray shot did hit a bottle of Martell Brandy in the General's staff car but there were no other casualties.

Before the rifle shots could stop echoing through the mountains, a Russian staff car roared up and skidded to a halt. "Don't shoot! Don't shoot! There is a Russian General here!" yelled an officer who sprang from the vehicle. Then Major-General Boris Alexeievich Holmston-Smyslonsky, Commander of the 1st Russian National Army, got out of the car and stepped forward. The well disciplined Russian soldiers stood at ease waiting to see what happened. The Grand Duke Vladimir Cyrillovich, great grandson of Tsar Alexander the Second, and Heir to the Throne of all the Russia's, sat quietly in another vehicle. After conferring with the General and ascertaining the Russians' intentions, the Police Officer telephoned his superior officer in Schaanwald, the main main border crossing.

After some consultation and negotiation, the Russians were allowed to enter the Principality. They were then disarmed peacefully and their weapons were locked up in Vaduz. Later the Swiss dumped them in the Bodensee.

While 462 men, 30 women and 2 children were given asylum, the Grand Duke and his immediate staff were returned to Austria next day. General Smyslovsky with his wife and staff were quartered in the Hotel Waldeck in Schellenberg. The soldiers were assigned two vacant schoolhouses while the women and children were placed in another hotel until more permanent housing could be found. The General was later transferred to the Hotel Lowe in Vaduz. The Liechtenstein Red Cross, founded in the same week by the Princess of Liechtenstein, raised money to help the refugees.

At first, the Liechtenstein Government was apprehensive that Communist dominated units in the 1st French Army might attempt a raid across the border to capture some of the Russian Generals. But the French Government, apparently aware of Liechtenstein's neutrality, quickly stepped in and prevented those units from carrying out their plan. But another danger arose. Other White Russian forces had surrendered to the allies or to the Soviets. Many were forcefully repatriated to Russia where they were summarily dealt with by the Communist authorities. General Smyslovsky, hoping to prevent the same happening to his people, sent on 10 May an appeal to His Highness to extend the humanitarian asylum to his people. The Prince and his people stood steadfast by the refugees insisting that only those who wanted to return willingly to Russia would go. Those, who did not want to go back, could stay in Liechtenstein.

In August, a contingent of Communist Officers from Russia arrived in Vaduz to demand that Liechtenstein hand over the Russian refugee soldiers. The Prince and his government refused only conceding that individual refugees were free to make their own decision as to whether to return to Russia or go to another country. While some allied countries like the United States, Great Britain forcefully repatriated Russian prisoners of war, Liechtenstein stood fast in its humanitarian resolve.

About 200 of the internees agreed to return to Russia where many were never heard from again. As for the others, they remained in Liechtenstein for a year. Then in the autumn of 1947, about 100 were accepted by Argentina.

In 1945, Liechtenstein's population was 12,141 and the country's annual budget was about two million Swiss francs. Yet the citizens of this little country provided without a single complaint 30,000 Swiss Francs to care for the Russian refugees. Tiny Liechtenstein, with no army and a eleven men police force did what no other European country dared. It defied the victorious Stalin in his demands for vengeance against Russian soldiers and their families who fought against him. Despite the fact that the Prince had vast property in Soviet dominated territory, he never waived in his resolve to do the right and humanitarian thing.

Liechtenstein was not pro-nazi in any way either, as some historians have suggested. After the collapse of Germany, Pierre Laval, Prime Minister of Vichy France, tried to enter Liechtenstein as a political refugee. Liechtenstein's Prime Minster personally went to the border and refused him entry. Laval returned to Austria and his ultimate fate.

INVASION SWISS STYLE

Switzerland accidentally attacked Liechtenstein three times in the last few years. In 1985, Swiss rockets, fired during an army exercise, landed in the Principality and set a forest on fire. The Swiss paid Liechtenstein preparations for the damage done.

On October 13, 1992, there occurred the military invasion of Liechtenstein, abet an accidental one! Switzerland, the Principality's neutral neighbor, briefly invaded Liechtenstein that Tuesday. Swiss troops, on maneuvers, had received orders to move to Triesenberg and set up camp. However, the Swiss forgot that Triesenberg was not on Swiss territory. The embarrassed troops quickly retired back across the border.

Then on March 1, 2007, one hundred and seventy Swiss soldiers armed with assault rifles but no ammunition wandered across the unmarked border between the two countries. When they realized their mistake, they quickly retreated. There were no apparent repercussions from that invasion.

POT POURIE
THE GOLDEN BOOS

In 1987 the Principality of Liechtenstein abolished the death penalty. The last person to be executed in the little country on 26 February, 1785 was a woman, known far and wide as the "Golden Boos". She was beheaded for her crimes. The Golden Boos' real name was Barbara Erni. She was born on 15 February, 1743, in Feldkirch to a homeless couple, Johann and Barbara Erni. In 1779, she married the well-known criminal "Tiroler Franz". Four of her five children did not survive infancy. Tired of being poor, Barbara developed a scheme to get rich at the expense of others. During six years of daring-do and illegal activity she became a legend, the "Golden Boos"! The name refers to her red-blond hair.

The Golden Boos, a woman of super-human strength, traveled about the countryside carrying a large wooden chest (a backpack some versions say). At whatever inn or farmhouse she stayed, she demanded that the chest be locked up in the best room. It contained a precious treasure, she claimed. Barbara must have had amazing powers of persuasion for people to believe that this strongly built woman possessed a treasure and to allow her to lock it where she choose. Instead of a treasure, it contained a secret. Inside was hidden a little man. The legend does not say whether or not it was her husband. During the night, when all were fast asleep, the little man crept out of his hiding place and made off with all the valuables of Barbara's host. The two thieves acquired a lot of money in this manner.

It was an ingenious scheme that worked for awhile. But, on one trip, she and presumably her little man were caught in Eschen and imprisoned at Vaduz on 27 May, 1784 . At her trial, the Golden Boos admitted to at least seventeen thefts. At this time, Liechtenstein, being a separate Principality, was a sort of safe haven for criminals from the surrounding domains. The Principality's judges decided that enough was enough and that an example had to be made. The Golden Boos was to be that example.

Barbara Erni, the legendary "Golden Boos", was condemned to death on 7 December, 1784. On 26 February, 1785, she taken out to the Rofenberg where a crowd of over a thousand people had gathered. The Landammann, the people's representative, broke a staff over her back. As Liechtenstein had no official executioner, one was imported. The hooded man swiftly beheaded the "Golden Boos".

The legend of Barbara Erni is today enshrined in the name of a road in Eschen, the Golden Boos Lane.

LAW AND EASY ORDER

In 1953, stories were told about the laxness of the Liechtenstein penal system. It was claimed that the best-behaved inmate was always trusted with the keys to the jail. Every evening, he would unlock his cell, go out to the local tavern to buy beer and food for his fellow inmates, return and lock himself back in. Many believe the story to be an exaggeration. The prison was apparently rarely used, as there was very little crime in the Principality. The story was thought to have started back in 1924 when the officials guilty of a great scandal were locked up there. Their relatives were allowed to bring things in when they visited.

COW COUNTRY

The year 1960 saw the Principality increase its credibility internationally and economically with its anticipation in the European Free Trade Association (EFTA). The first time visitor to the little country and particularly Vaduz, the capital village, at that time, would have been amazed to see the large number of cows roaming around. In the early morning, they wandered freely through the streets on their way to grazing in the alpine slopes up in the Alps. In the evening they invaded the streets and roads again heading back to their barns. Indeed they often blocked traffic at any time during the day. Few people bothered about them as cattle raising has been a staple of the Liechtenstein economy for centuries. There was recorded that year, 8116 head of cattle owned by 862 farmers. With only 15000 people living in the Principality that year (1960) that would make it one cow per two persons. The number of chickens in the country is even greater. Over 33,000 are raised annually in the little country.

THE THREE SISTERS

Above the village of Planked at Gafadura, three large rock formations called the Three Sisters can be found there. This is their story about how they came to be there and why they got their name. Years ago, three sisters went went up the mountain to pick berries on of all days , the Feast of the Assumption on 15 August. They heard the church bells calling the faithful to worship. One sister suggested that they should go back and attend church but the other two persuaded her to continue with them. When their baskets were full, they started back down the mountain. On their way, they met a beautiful woman who asked for some of their berries. The three sisters replied insolently that if she wanted berries, she should pick them herself. Well, imagine their surprise, when a halo appeared around the beautiful woman's head and she admonished them for not keeping her holy day and for refusing her request. Then she declared that their hearts were of stone. There and then on that spot she turned the three sisters to stone. Now for eternity they sit there as big rocks.

FUNKENSONNTAF (SPARK SUNDAY)

When it is spring in Liechtenstein, it's time to drive away the winter blahs! Liechtensteiners follow a custom that is still practiced in other German-speaking countries such as Austria and Germany. On the first Sunday of Lent, just after Ash Wednesday, the inhabitants of each village in the Principality burn a huge wooden tower with an effigy of a witch that they had previously erected. In this way, they drive away the dark spirits of winter and welcome the warm, cheerful days of spring. The custom gets it name, Funkensonntag –

Spark Sunday from the sparks flying off from the roaring flames in the night sky.

On the Tuesday before Ash Wednesday, the villagers search out fir trees and cut them down into lengths of up to 30 meters. The fir gives off a lot of sparks when burned. On the Saturday before Spark Sunday, they build the wooden tower. A large life-like doll, meant to represent a witch, is attached to the top of the structure. In other countries, gunpowder or fireworks are placed in the witch so that when the witch catches fire it explodes. The tower is lit as soon as it gets dark and all the villagers gather around to watch. Sometimes the children carry lanterns and a band stands by waiting for the witch to catch fire before they begin playing.

Local legend says that the more quickly the fire burns, the hotter the spring will be. I wonder what it means if it rains on Spark Sunday and the fire can not burn? A long wet spring?

The first historical reference to the custom occurs in a report of the Benediktinerklosters Lorsch, when the monastery was apparently set on fire by a burning wood disk in the evening of March 21, 1090, AD. The Christians do not, they say, relate the Funkensonntag to the terrible witch trials and burnings of the Middle Ages but believe it is an adaptation of an old pagan custom when Christianity was introduced into the region. Some claim it is a ceremony from a Germanic spring cult or New Year celebration and is connected with spring cleaning of houses and meadows. Whatever its origin, the custom in Liechtenstein is a time of great celebration and competition between villages to see who can build the largest wooden tower. In 1995 the record was set at 25 meters high.

Sometimes the contest can get a little tense. In an effort to cut the competition down to size, so to speak, inhabitants of a village would often burn the tower of a nearby village a few days before Funkensonntag. Another favorite tactic was to steal someone else's witch.

Whether they have the tallest wooden tower, and whether or not the fire burns quickly, the citizens of Liechtenstein have a great time on Spark Sunday chasing away their winter blahs.

CHRISTMAS IN LICHTENSTEIN

In Liechtenstein, the Christmas season starts around December 6th or 7th. St. Nicholas or Santa Claus, usually a family member or friend in costume, visits each household and tells the children who have been good and who has been bad. Then the children tell him what they want the Christmas Angel to bring them on Christmas Eve. In Liechtenstein, it is an angel, the "Christkindli", and not Santa Claus who makes the gifts magically appear under the Christmas Tree.

The Christmas Tree is brought home about two weeks before Christmas. On Christmas Eve, the tree is decorated and they put out their presents that they brought. Then the children are off to bed and are all excited as to what the "Christkindli" might bring them. Some families open their presents on Christmas Eve or on Christmas Day. Christmas is also a time to visit relatives in other villages and to exchange greetings and presents.

Their Christmas is similar in most ways to the ones I remember from my childhood. I can imagine being in Triesenberg on Christmas Eve with snow softly falling. Can you hear the Christmas carols sung in German? "O Tannenbaum O Tannenbaum". Can you hear the excited laughter of children? Can you feel the magic? I am starting to once again, thanks to the magic of Christmas in Liechtenstein!

(The above information was provided in an email from a member of a family in Liechtenstein that I met one summer in Vancouver, British Columbia. Nicole Gassner of Triesenberg told me how they celebrate Christmas there. Thank you, Nicole.)

MY GIFT TO THE PEOPLE OF LIECHTENSTEIN

THE CHRISTMAS ANGEL AND THE GIANT

Public Domain Image as per http://store.tidbitstrinkets.com/blog/?tag=angel

In the mountains above the village of Vaduz in the Principality of Liechtenstein lies a small village. Many years ago, a family lived on the edges of that village in their little farm house. There was a father and mother, and their twin children, Karl and Gretchen, who were about ten years old at the time of this story. The family raised goats as well as planting and harvesting potatoes and other vegetables in a plot near the house. The cheese they made from the goats milk was delicious and brought by many of their neighbors. They had just enough to make their lives comfortable with some left over to sell to buy a few extra things from the trader who occasionally found his way up to the little village.

This one year, in late summer, the father took sick and was unable to do his work. The mother and the twins tried to harvest the potatoes and the other vegetables, as well as herd the goats in the pastures, milk them and make the cheese. Thus, it was with sadness that the family one night settled down to sleep. They were completely exhausted from their hard work, unable to finish it. They had milked the goats but were unable to make the cheese. The potatoes still lay in the ground and would soon rot if not harvested. The father lay sick on his bed unable to rise. They needed to make the cheese to sell to get money so that they could go down to the valley below and buy medicine. They all slept fitfully that night.

Little Karl was the first up that morning and he went out to let the goats out to pasture. Within minutes, he came running back in calling for his mother. The goats! The goats were gone!

His mother and sister rushed outside and, to their horror, they found that Karl was right. The goats were not in the shed. They were gone. The mother looked frantically around for them. Then she spied them up on the pastures grazing merrily away. Somehow they had gotten out and found their way to the pasture. They gave thanks to the Virgin Mary and to God.

Then they noticed that all their vegetables were gone from their garden patch. "Thieves!" they cried out. Then they noticed the baskets piled near the barn door were full of vegetables. Someone had harvested them during the night.

They also noticed that a small portion was missing. Nevertheless, once again they gave thanks to God and the Virgin Mary as well as to whoever had helped them.

Next they checked the goats milk and to their amazement they found that it had been made into cheese. Here also they noticed that a small portion was missing. It was a small price to pay for the miracle. For the third time they gave thanks to God and the Virgin Mary as well as to whoever had helped them. Then, the mother took the cheese down to the village, sold it and then got medicine for her husband. With the help of the medicine, the father soon got well.

But until he did, the wife and twins labored hard to get the work done but there was always something not finished. Every morning they would wake up to find the work completed by someone unknown during the night. They were always too tired to stay up to see who it was. But they blessed their unknown benefactor, who ever it was.

Then, early one morning, Gretchen awoke to sounds of the goats' bell. Immediately she peaked out the window. To her amazement, she saw a giant leading the goats out to pasture. She woke her brother who also saw the giant. But when they woke their mother and father to show them, the giant had gone. They told their parents what they saw and their parents smiled knowingly. There had been rumors about a giant living in the mountains but no one had as yet seen him. People had found chores, unfinished the night before done the following morning. And always a small portion was taken in payment.

That day their father was well enough to go back to work. There was no need now for their benefactor but they did not forget him. They always left something out for him at night and in the morning it was gone. In its place would be berries and mushrooms gather from high up in normally inaccessible mountains valleys.

As late summer turned into autumn and the leaves turned their many colors, the twins kept an eye out for their giant friend. Many of the other children made fun of them behind their backs. They did not believe in giants. They existed only in stories they said. But Gretchan and Karl both knew better.

Then, with the first snow of winter, the giant failed to stop by at night and pick up the little gifts they left for him. When they told their father, he shook his head and said that maybe the fellow had moved on to warmer climes. Their mother just smiled and replied that maybe he would be back in the spring. Neither were right.

The giant, one night, had over heard two men talking as they left a tavern. They did not believe in the giant but thought that if they could capture him and take him to the Prince's men at the Castle in Vaduz, maybe they could get a reward. The giant listened carefully to their plans and decided not to visit the farms anymore. He quietly retreated up to his cave high up in the mountains where few people dared to go. There, as snow began to fall, the giant settled down to a long and lonely winter. He had stocked enough food to tide him over the winter and had gathered enough firewood to keep himself warmth. But he was sad as he like going down to the lower slopes and helping the people with their chores. That way, he felt like he belonged somewhere instead of living alone in the high mountains. Now he would have to stay hidden alone in the mountains for his own safety.

The snow continued to fall covering the peaks and slopes all the way down to the villages along the Rhine River. Christmas was beginning to approach and all the people of the little village began to prepare for festivities. They celebrate Christmas a bit different in Liechtenstein.

The Christmas season starts around December 6th or 7th in the Principality. A friend or family member, dressed as St. Nicholas or Santa Claus, visits each home and tells the children who have been good and who has been bad. The gleeful children then tell St. Nicholas what they want the "Christkindli", the Christmas Angel, to bring them on Christmas Eve. It is an angel, and not Santa Claus, who brings presents on Christmas Eve. Two weeks before Christmas, the tree is set up. It is decorated on Christmas Eve and presents are put under it, ready for the coming Christmas morning.

In the excitement of the festive season, the giant and his good deeds were soon forgotten. But not by two children. Gretchen and Karl remembered and each made a pecial Christmass present for the giant. Karl carved a toy soldier out of pine wood while Gretchen embroidered a small piece of Lace with a Christmas scene. They continued to leave food out for the giant but he never returned to claim the food. They began to worry that something had happened to the giant. Their parents, while concerned, tried to placate them with the thought that the giant had moved on to warmer climes. But the children knew better. Once in a while, they thought that they had caught glimpses of him high up on the snow-covered slopes. In the innocent way of children, they wondered what he was going to do for Christmas, all alone up there in the cold and snow. Would the Christmas Angel also visit him?

St. Nicholas came and visited all the children. Everyone went out and got their Christmas tree.

The Day before Christmas arrived and the twins went out to play with some friends on the other side of the village. At least that is what they told their parents. But the children had a plan. They had secretly brought their gifts for the giant and planned to seek out the giant's cave while their father chopped and trimmed the tree. They knew from listening to the old men telling tales around the fireside at night that it was commonly thought the giant had taken up residence in one of the caves on the upper slopes above the village. The twins planned to look for the cave that day and leave their presents there for the giant. They were sure that it was just up the mountain a ways and they would be back well before dark. The children quickly disappeared up the snow -covered tree slope and just as quickly became lost.

When night came and the twins had not returned, their parents became very worried. The snow had been falling heavily all day. The father checked with the neighbor's kids and found that they had never shown up. He roused the villagers and with lighted torches, they ventured as far into the mountains as they dared searching for the children, calling out their names. They returned to the village after several hours tired, hungry, cold and wet. Out of hearing of the twins' parents, some suggested that perhaps the giant got them. They shook their heads and went back to their warm, dry homes.

The children, meanwhile, realizing that they were lost, tried to head back downhill, but somehow ended up in a little alpine valley. The falling snow became too deep for them to go any farther. They settled down in a sheltered spot like their father had taught them and huddled together to keep warm. They prayed to the Virgin Mary that their parents would find them soon.

The giant sat in his dry cave before a blazing fire. His thoughts wandered to his childhood when he had grew faster and taller than all the other children in his faraway village. By his teens, he was nearly 8 feet tall. When his parents died, the villagers, fearful of his size and strength, drove him out of the village. But he was a gentle giant and did not resist. He moved on from village to village looking for a place that would accept him for himself and let him live there in peace.

As he sat before the warm fire, this Christmas Eve, a silver green glow seethed in through the entrance to his cave. The strange light moved softly into the main cavern, and, hovering in the air, resolved into the vision of an angel.

"The Christkindli", whispered the giant in awe!

"Come", spoke the Christmas Angel. "The children have need of you". The giant followed the shinning light out into the snow and cold. It let him down the mountain slope to a small alpine valley. There, the light hovered over two small nearly frozen figures. The giant gathered them up in his arms and took them to his cave.

Down in the village, the twins' father would periodically go outside with a torch and call out his children's names in the hopes that they would somehow hear it and find their way safely home. His wife knelt inside at the family alter praying to the Virgin Mary for the safe return of her children. The father, totally exhausted, turned to go inside, when he noticed a bright green light moving through the falling snow on the mountain side. Amazed, he watched it draw closer. He called to his wife to come and see the sight! She rushed out to join her husband. Other villagers, hearing the commotion, also came out into the snowy night. And lo, they all beheld the Christkindli in the midst of the light and fell to their knees in reverence. And to all their amazement, a giant loomed out of the falling snow. The twins, smiling and laughing, rode on his shoulders.

"A miracle!" whispered their mother. "Thanks be to the Virgin Mary and God!" The giant set the children down and stepped back wary of the villagers who now gathered about the happy parents and their children. Some of the men were beginning to look suspiciously at the giant.

Then, the bright light floated to the top of a pine tree in the middle of the village. A shimmering light descended from it covering the whole tree. At the top, a star appeared while the snow crystals on its branches began to glitter in many different colors like ornaments on a Christmas Tree.

"Lo, on to you a child is born this day!" came an angelic voice from sky.

All the villagers stood in shock and awe. Then the father of the two twins stepped forward and offered his hand to the giant.

"Thank you for saving our children. It is the best Christmas present anyone could have given us. You are welcome in our home for as long as you wish. Come in and warm yourself." He motioned towards his home. His wife nodded in agreement. The twins each grabbed a hand of the giant and laughingly pulled him inside. The villagers all cheered!

That Christmas in the little village on the slopes of the Liechtenstein Alps was one of the best for the whole village and especially the giant. He now had a home and he lived with the family happily ever after.

REFERENCES:

BOOKS

Greene, Barbara, Liechtenstein/Valley of Peace, Liechtenstein-Verlag, Vaduz, 1967

Moore, Russell F., Principality Of Liechtenstein/A Brief History, Simmons-Boardman Publishing Corp, New York, 1960

Raton, Pierre, Liechtenstein/History and Institutions of the Principality, Liechtenstein-Verlag, Vaduz, 1970

Reichler, Claude, How Dragons Disappeared from the Alps in the Mid-Eighteenth Century, Abstract from "Reconceptualizing Nature, Science, and Aesthetics", ed. by P. Coleman, A. Hofmann, S. Zurbuchen, Slatkine ed., Geneva, 1998; English translation by Julia Gallagher. http://www2. unil.ch/acvs/E/publ_0099.html

Schlapp, Manfred, This is Liechtenstein, Seewald Publishing Company, Stuttgart, 1980

Vonbun, Franz Jose, fThe legends Vorarlbergs. With contributions from Liechtenstein, NR. 203

Walser, H.F., Liechtenstein/Land of Legend, QUICK, Vaduz, Li., May 1957, a translation by Esmee Mascall of "Sagenumwobene Heimats" by .

INTERNET

facstaff.uww.edu/rambadtd/Alpine/

www.bng.nl/ngw

www.dfat.gov.au/geo/liechtenstein/liechtenstein_brief.html

http://www.everything2.com/

www.eye.ch/swissgen/FL/flemi1-e.h...

www.frommers.com/destinations/liewww.geocities.com/Tokyo/Temple/26

www.liechtenstein.li/lisite/html/liechtenstein/

www.tourismus.li/en/culture-cuisine/Liechtenstein-legends-
fables/Lichtenstein-fables/fable-2.html
www.maurenonline.li/about.asp?str

www.mcowls.li/Liechtenstein1.htm

www.mtsd.k12.wi.us/MTSD/Homestead

www.newadvent.org/cathen/14358a.htm

www.philately.com/philately/liech...

www.public.asu.edu/~goutam/gcu325...

www.silvancolani.com/navy/navyhome.html The Liechtenstein Princely Navy

www.snikt.com/Timeline_of_History/AD/1401--1500/1403.htm

www.supra.net/haebi/index.html Herbert Hilbe home page

www.tourismus.li/en/culture-cuisine/Liechtenstein-legends-
fables/Lichtenstein-fables/

www.unterland.li/state/ruggell.htm

OTHER

Nicole Gassner, Triesenberg, Liechtenstein, email

Document of Johann Ernst Varnbüler born 2 March 1850, English translation of a German document that outlines a possible early history of the Varnbüler family. The family Varnbueler Website

"The Rhine In Liechtenstein" was published on November 24, 2002 at www.suite101.com/article.cfm/15314/96245

The Mals Dragon was told about in a previous article "Halloween Tales from Liechtenstein" at http://www.suite101.com/article.cfm/liechtenstein/83455

ABOUT THE AUTHOR

James Foster Robinson was born in Ogdensburg, New York, USA but grew up in Prescott, Ontario, Canada. He has lived and worked in Ontario, Manitoba, Alberta and . In 2005, he moved to West Virginia and married his present wife, Betty. Jim has two books published by Mika Publishing, Belleville, Ontario Amazing Tales from Eastern Ontario, 1987; Strange But True Tales From Eastern Ontario, 1989. He has also published numerous articles in national magazines, daily and weekly newspapers. While living in Vancouver, BC, Jim was a Feature Writer on Suite101.com for topics - The Art of Storytelling, Storyteller's Korner, Sleep Disorders, Professional Security, and Liechtenstein. In addition, he was a Storyteller both in Kingston, Ontario and in Vancouver, BC, Canada. James has also published "A Ghostly Guide to West Virginia", "West Virginia Weird and Wonderful", "An Encyclopedia of Lake and River Monsters", "Riotous Times, An Unauthorized History of Riots and Violent Protests in British Columbia, Canada", "A Ghostly Guide to Kentucky", "A Ghostly Guide to California", "The Wampus Cat, Myth or Reality", "Sleep Dancing With Death/Struggling with Sleep Apnea", "Storytelling for Fun", "Are They Ghosts?", "British Columbia Weird" and a children book "Tales To Tell My Children", a novel "Umpock - The Hole In The Ground", "Ghost Lights, Spook Lights, Will o' Wisps and Friends" and his latest book "Gravity, Magical, Magnetic and Spook Hills Around The World" on Amazon.com. He is presently working on Ghostly Guides to the remaining 46 states and the 10 provinces of Canada.

www.ingramcontent.com/pod-product-compliance
Lightning Source LLC
Chambersburg PA
CBHW081837280526
45789CB00007B/2482